HO Scale
Model Railroading

Getting Started in the Hobby

Jeff Wilson

KALMBACH
BOOKS

Contents

1   **Basics of HO Scale**   **7**

2   **Basic Tool Set**   **12**

3   **Couplers**   **17**

4   **Wheels and Trucks**   **24**

5   **Maintaining Locomotives**   **29**

6   **Building and Upgrading Freight Cars**   **33**

7   **Benchwork**   **41**

Printed in the United States of America

03 04 05 06 07 08 09 10 11 12   10 9 8 7 6 5 4 3 2 1

Visit our website at http://kalmbachbooks.com
Secure online ordering available

Publisher's Cataloging-in-Publication
(Provided by Quality Books, Inc.)

Wilson, Jeff, 1964-
    HO scale model railroading : getting started in the hobby / Jeff Wilson.
    p. cm.
    Includes index.
    ISBN 0-89024-575-4

    1. Railroads—Models. I. Title.

  TF197.W49825 2003   625.1'9
                     QBI03-200261

Art director: Kristi Ludwig
Book design: Sabine Beaupré

8   Roadbed   44

9   Track   47

10 Wiring   59

11 Structures   72

12 Basic Scenery   80

    Trackside Photos   89

    Suppliers and Manufacturers   95

    Index   96

chapter one

Basics of HO Scale

Welcome to the hobby of model railroading! Ours has been a popular pastime since the early 20th century, and for good reason. Model railroading is a multifaceted hobby that goes beyond simply playing with trains. In fact, the trains are but one part of the hobby.

Many modelers find their main interest lies in modeling realistic scenery and structures. Others enjoy painting and detailing locomotives and freight cars to match real ones. Still others enjoy re-creating the operations of real railroads, and many delve into history, doing extensive research on specific railroads and their operations and equipment.

Why choose HO scale? For starters, the variety of models and accessories available in HO is much larger than in any other scale. You'll find models of almost every diesel locomotive and a wide range of steam locomotives, as well as a tremendous variety of rolling stock, structure kits, and detail items.

Modeling in HO gives you the option of buying models ready-to-run or in kit form. The number of assembled models that are commercially available has increased greatly in recent years, but you'll also find many master modelers who scratchbuild (our term for building something from raw components) or extensively modify and detail their models to match specific real (we call them "prototype") trains.

Its size makes HO popular, as it's relatively easy to add detail parts to models ("superdetail" them). More details are available in HO than in other scales, and these details are easier to see and model realistically than in smaller scales.

Fig. 1-1. This HO scale Proto 2000 locomotive (right) is roughly twice as big in each dimension as its Kato N scale cousin. Both are models of E8 passenger diesels.

You can fit almost four times as much railroading into a given area in HO as in O scale, since a 4 x 8-foot layout would take close to 8 x 16 feet in O scale.

HO models are $\frac{1}{87}$ the real thing (to be precise, the proportion is 1:87.1, but it's generally rounded to 1:87). Thus, a real foot (12 inches) in HO scale is .138″, or 3.5 mm. Don't worry, though—

Fig. 1-2. This Life-Like set includes a locomotive, two freight cars and a caboose, a loop of track, a power pack, and a detail set.

Fig. 1-3. This set from Atlas consists of a high-quality locomotive and cars, together with an oval of track, a power pack, and a small structure kit.

fancy calculations aren't necessary. Simply buy yourself a scale rule (see Chapter 2) and you'll be able to make the translation easily.

It's important to understand the distinction between scale and gauge. Scale is the proportion of the models to the real thing—in the case of HO, 1:87.1. Gauge is the distance between the rails. Thus, a structure can't be HO gauge, but it can be HO scale.

The initials HO come from "half O," since HO scale is roughly half of O scale (1:48), which was the dominant scale among modelers through the 1940s. In the late 1940s and through the 1950s, smaller motors and other components made smaller scales practical. Other common modeling scales are N (1:160) and S (1:64), as well as large scale (ranging from 1:20.1 to 1:32). Figure 1-1 shows an HO model next to an N scale one.

Getting started

There are many ways to get started in modeling. Perhaps you've already bought or been given an HO scale train set, or maybe you've seen HO models (or perhaps a complete model railroad) at a friend's home, train club open house, or public display.

A train set can be a good way to get started in the hobby. Most train sets include all you need to get a train running: a locomotive, a few freight cars and a caboose, a loop of track, and a power pack.

Model railroading sets come in a wide variety of sizes and prices. What should you look for when buying one? Like many other products, train sets range in quality from excellent to poor. And, although there are exceptions, you generally get what you pay for: Few $30 train sets will run as well or look as good as those costing $100.

Figure 1-2 shows an inexpensive train set from Life-Like; fig. 1-3 shows a high-quality set from Atlas. Both include a locomotive, three freight cars, an oval of track, and a power pack. The Atlas set also includes a small structure kit, and the Life-Like set has a set of signs and telephone poles. However, the Atlas set costs significantly more.

The main difference is in the locomotives. The Atlas set includes a diesel switcher from the firm's standard line (fig. 1-4). It has a good-quality motor and a heavy die-cast frame. It picks up electricity from all eight wheels, and all four axles are powered. The shell is quite realistic, and it is painted in a paint scheme accurate for a specific prototype railroad.

The Life-Like engine in fig. 1-5 has a simple, light frame with a small motor mounted on, and powering, only one truck (the frame that holds the wheelsets). The shell doesn't have as high a level of detail as the Atlas engine, and the paint scheme isn't

Fig. 1-4. This Atlas engine is a high-quality, realistic model with all axles powered.

Fig. 1-5. The Life-Like train set engine has an inexpensive motor that powers only one truck. It also isn't as nicely detailed as the Atlas model.

Seven tips for beginners

1. Read. No single magazine or book can cover every aspect of modeling in depth. Kalmbach Publishing Co. offers dozens of books on specific areas of the hobby, including scenery, wiring, painting, and others. Kalmbach also publishes the leading magazine in the hobby, *Model Railroader*. In addition, there are many other magazines and books from other publishers. Read as many as you can.

2. Start small. Many new modelers, filled with enthusiasm, are tempted to begin by filling a basement with a model railroad empire. However, starting with a small layout (4 x 8 feet or less) lets you try all facets of the hobby (trackwork, scenery, structures, wiring, detailing) in short order. It's also easy to fix mistakes (or even start over again) on a small layout.

3. Visit a hobby shop. Browsing through a well-stocked hobby shop will give you lots of ideas. It's the best way to see the wide range of products available, view models of different eras, and see the many paint schemes. Also, many hobby shops tend to be gathering places for modelers, making shops a great place to learn from others.

4. Get your trains off the floor. It can be fun to run trains on the floor, but moving them off the carpeting and onto a table will improve operations, lessen the risk of damage, and make it easier to try track arrangements and add other items such as structures.

5. Become active. Start a project—perhaps a structure or car kit—and continue it through to completion without worrying if it turns out perfectly. If your first efforts aren't what you'd hoped for, try again. Keep in mind that it takes time and practice to become proficient in model railroading, like any physical activity.

6. Start with a published track plan. When you're ready to build your first "real" layout, start with a plan from a book or magazine. Keep it simple—a loop of track with a couple of sidings and spurs will provide lots of operating interest.

7. Have fun. It can be easy to get frustrated when something doesn't turn out as planned. Remember that the only reason to have a hobby is fun, and the only person you have to please is yourself. There's no "right" way to do it. There are so many interesting facets to the hobby that you'll easily gravitate to the ones you enjoy the most.

accurate (real F40PH diesels were passenger locomotives, and the Union Pacific never had any).

Next, look at the freight cars. The Atlas cars—once again from the firm's standard line of cars—have metal wheels, lots of separately added details, and accurate, sharp paint schemes. See fig. 1-6. The body and truck detailing is very good.

The Life-Like cars (fig. 1-7) have plastic wheels in snap-fit trucks, and the details are molded in place on the shells. The paint schemes aren't as realistic as those of the Atlas set.

The power pack supplied in the Atlas set is also a higher-quality item.

Many of these differences, such as the accuracy of paint schemes and depth of detail, might not be apparent to you if you're just getting into the hobby. However, as you gain experience, chances are you'll eventually take more notice of realism.

This isn't a knock against Life-Like—as you see in fig. 1-1 (and you'll see later in this book) the firm's Proto 2000 line includes some of the best products in the hobby today. It's just that this particular set isn't designed for the higher end of the market.

Fig. 1-6. The Atlas cars, from the firm's standard line, have excellent detailing, metal wheels, and body-mounted couplers.

Fig. 1-7. The Life-Like train set cars have molded-on detail and snap-on trucks with truck-mounted couplers.

Good-quality train sets are available from Athearn, Atlas, Life-Like Proto 1000 and Proto 2000, and Walthers (Trainline).

Building your own set

You can also put together your own set. Although this can be a slightly more expensive option, it allows you to get the exact locomotive and freight cars that you prefer instead of settling for some components you don't really want.

Start with a ready-to-run locomotive from Athearn, Atlas, or Life-Like Proto 1000 or Proto 2000. Add four or five ready-to-run freight cars from Athearn, Atlas, Proto 2000, InterMountain, or Kadee, with a caboose of the same road name as the locomotive.

Add an oval of track from Atlas and a power pack from Model Rectifier Corp., and you'll have a set that will operate reliably. You'll also have equipment that you can continue to use as you expand your collection and build a permanent layout.

Getting set up

Many sets are initially set up on the living room carpet, as fig. 1-8 shows. Although it's a tempting choice, carpeting is not the ideal spot for HO trains. Carpet fibers and dust can easily get into locomotive gears, hampering operations. Also, carpeting doesn't provide a firm base for the track, and things on floors tend to get stepped on.

Using one of the combination track/roadbed products, such as the Atlas True-Track or Life-Like Power-Loc track certainly helps. The best solution, however, is to get the trains onto a table—even if it's just a piece of plywood laid across a pair of sawhorses.

A permanent table or structure with trains and scenery is known as a layout. The permanent table or structure itself is called benchwork. Having a table devoted strictly to trains allows you to add details such as structures, roads, trees, rivers, ballast, and other elements, creating a realistic setting for your trains. Figure 1-9 shows an excellent example of a good small layout.

The following chapters will help get you started, providing guidance in maintaining and building locomotives, freight cars, and structures; laying reliable trackwork; and making basic scenic terrain. Let's get started!

Fig. 1-8. The floor can be a handy spot to set up trains and experiment with track arrangements, but it's better to get trains off the floor and onto a table.

Fig. 1-9. Maggie's Cove is a beautiful 4 x 8-foot HO layout. It includes an oval of track with two spurs, a river, a beach, bridges, a tunnel, a small town, a crossing, and lots of detail. It shows what can be accomplished in a relatively small area.

chapter two

Basic Tool Set

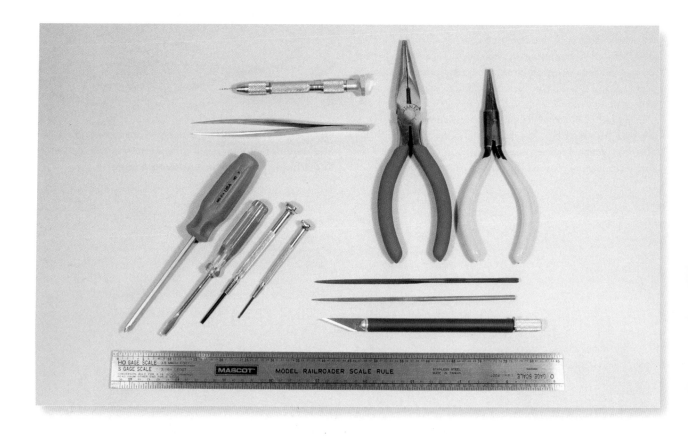

Working on locomotives, structures, and other model railroading

equipment requires many small and specialized tools. Some are

miniature versions of common workshop tools; others are tools specific

to the hobby. Let's start by looking at a basic tool set.

Basic tools

These tools are those that I feel are essential for modeling. You might be able to get by without some of them, but they aren't expensive, and they will enable you to do a good job of building kits, repairing cars and locomotives, adding details, adding couplers, and performing many other tasks.

Start with a good hobby knife. Once you begin modeling, you'll find yourself using a hobby knife more than any other tool. Many different handle and blade styles are available. Find a handle that fits comfortably in your hand, then buy two of them. Keep a no. 11 (pointed) blade on one and a no. 17 (chisel-tip) blade on the other. See fig. 2-1.

You'll use the pointed blade for cutting plastic, wood, paper, and other materials, in addition to carving mold flash from models. The no. 17 blade works well for cutting plastic and wood parts from sprues as well as chopping strip materials.

Always use sharp blades. As soon as the tip breaks or the blade begins to become dull, replace it with a fresh blade. Dull blades tend to tear material, require excess pressure to use, and are much more likely to slip and cause injury.

Buy blades in bulk packs. They're much more economical to purchase this way, and you're much more likely to use a fresh blade if you have a plentiful supply. See fig. 2-2.

Don't simply throw used blades in the garbage—protect yourself and your garbage collector by putting them in a sealed plastic container (such as the old film canister in fig. 2-2). You can also buy sharps disposal containers designed specifically for this purpose.

A scale rule is next on the list. Perhaps the handiest is the 12″-long (87-scale-foot) steel variety, as in fig. 2-3. This is not only handy for measuring, but it serves as a straightedge and guide for a hobby knife. Most scale rules have both HO and N scale markings; others have additional scales as well. Even if you model strictly in HO, you'll find it handy to have rules in other scales for transferring dimensions from drawings done in another scale.

Clear plastic rules (fig. 2-4) are also handy, especially in taking measurements from drawings—they enable you to see details of the drawing through the rule. They're also handy for taking measurements directly from models.

Tweezers work well for grabbing and moving small parts. Standard straight-tipped and curved-tip tweezers (fig. 2-5) are

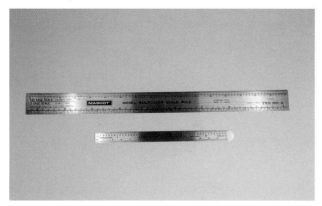

Fig. 2-1. Knives with no. 11 (top) and no. 17 (bottom) blades are both handy.

Fig. 2-2. Bulk packs (such as this box of 100 X-Acto no. 11 blades) are economical. Place old blades in a sealed plastic container.

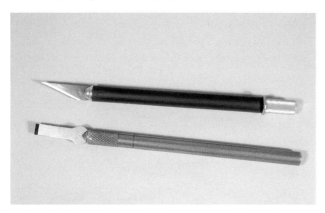

Fig. 2-3. A foot-long steel scale rule is among the most essential tools. A shorter rule with inch and millimeter markings is also handy.

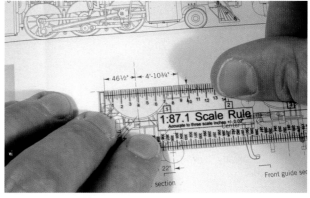

Fig. 2-4. See-through rules, like this one from Scale Card, are handy for measuring drawings and models.

both handy. Look for tweezers with fine, sharp points. Avoid those with rounded tips or points that are misaligned.

Tweezers are easily damaged. If they fall to the floor, the tips can become bent. It is sometimes possible to reshape them with pliers, but it's usually better to just replace them.

Needle files are used to clean, smooth, and shape plastic, metal, wood, and other materials. Figure 2-6 shows several. You'll find flat, square, and round needle files all handy.

Needle-nose pliers have fine tips. They can hold parts and get into small spaces that standard pliers can't. Figure 2-7 shows a few varieties, from small to medium-sized. They can be used to shape wire and metal, hold onto parts during kit construction, and grab parts in tight places.

A set of jeweler's screwdrivers will prove handy, as will small and medium-sized Phillips and slotted screwdrivers. See fig. 2-8. Be sure to use the proper size bit for any given screw. Using a screwdriver that's too small will damage the bit or may cause the screwdriver to slip and damage the model.

Don't use screwdrivers as chisels or pry bars. This can bend and chip the tip, making it useless for its intended purpose.

Some consider a pin vise and drill bits (fig. 2-9) to be advanced tools, but I place them in the basic category. A pin vise is basically a small manual drill driver. It can be used to drill holes in plastic, wood, and soft metal.

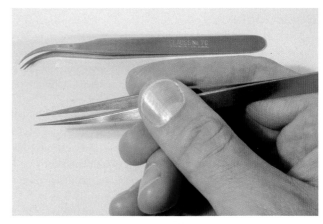

Fig. 2-5. Make sure tweezers have sharp points that match each other well.

Sizes of small drill bits are indicated by number: the higher the number, the smaller the bit. In modeling we most often use sizes from no. 61 (.040″) to no. 80 (.0135″). I suggest buying a set of nos. 61 to 80 bits (see fig. 2-9), along with nos. 50 and 43 bits, which are often used in coupler installation. Replace bits as they break or become worn.

The key to drilling a hole with a pin vise is to let the bit do the work—don't apply any more pressure than is required to hold the

Fig. 2-6. Needle files (or jeweler's files) are available in many shapes.

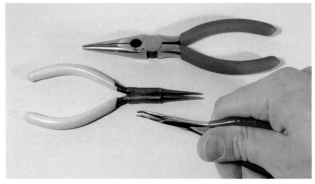

Fig. 2-7. Needle-nose pliers in different sizes are handy for grasping small parts.

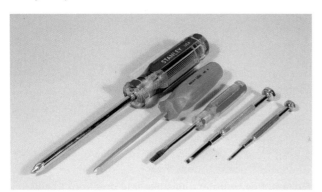

Fig. 2-8. You'll need small screwdrivers with both standard and Phillips tips.

Fig. 2-9. A pin vise is a handy tool for drilling holes with small (nos. 61 to 80) bits.

bit in place. While working, pull the bit out of the hole frequently to clear material.

Flush sprue cutters (fig. 2-10) are the handiest tool for removing plastic parts from their sprues. They cut parts more cleanly than do hobby knives, so no touchup is usually necessary. These cutters (available from JBL and Micro-Mark) can be expensive, but you'll find them well worth the price if you build a lot of plastic kits.

Adhesives

Using the correct adhesive will result in a sturdy bond and a solid model. Using the wrong adhesive can make the construction weak, damage parts, and leave blemishes. Figure 2-11 shows several adhesives.

Liquid plastic cement (solvent) is the proper choice for most plastic-to-plastic joints. Plastic cement works by melting the plastic surface on the joining parts, allowing them to fuse together to form an extremely strong joint.

Two types are available: thin liquids that are applied with a brush, such as Testor's no. 3502, Tenax 7R, and Plastruct Plastic Weld; and thicker cements, such as Model Master no. 8872 and Testor's no. 3507, which use built-in needle-point applicators.

The following chapters show examples of using each of these products. In general, use liquid when you have a tight joint, especially when you can apply the adhesive from behind. Applying it with a brush to the joint allows capillary action to pull it into the joint. Use thick cement when pressing mating surfaces together or when joining separate parts.

In either case, hold the mating surfaces together for several seconds while the glue goes to work. If the joint is a forced one, and one piece tends to pull away from the other, clamp the pieces together overnight to let the glue joint cure.

It's important that mating surfaces be clear of paint before you apply plastic cement; otherwise, the joint will be weak. Use the edge of a hobby knife to scrape paint away.

Because plastic cements work by solvent action, they won't work on anything but plastic—don't use them on metal, wood, resin, or other materials.

Cyanoacrylate adhesive (CA), also known as super glue, works well for joining dissimilar materials such as plastic, metal, and wood. It's ideal for nonporous materials.

Cyanoacrylate adhesive is available in several thicknesses, or viscosities, with thin, medium, and thick the most common. Thin is as it sounds—it has a consistency and surface tension thinner than water and is appropriate only for joints that are very tight. The bonding time is almost instantaneous: Make the joint, add a touch of thin CA to the joint, and capillary action will draw it in. Examples of thin CA are Instant Jet, UFO Thin, and Zap CA.

Medium-viscosity is the best general-purpose CA. Greater thickness makes it easier to handle than thin CA, but it still cures fairly quickly—usually in 5 to 15 seconds. For small applications, squeeze a few drops of CA onto a piece of scrap plastic and use the tip of a toothpick to apply it. Examples of medium CA products include Insta Cure and Super Jet.

Thick CA (sometimes with fillers labeled as "gap-filling")

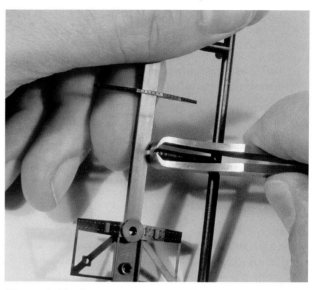

Fig. 2-10. Flush sprue cutters are designed to trim parts cleanly.

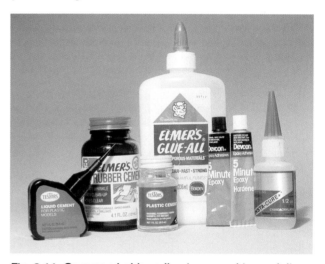

Fig. 2-11. Common hobby adhesives used in modeling include thick liquid plastic cement, rubber cement, thin liquid plastic cement, white glue, epoxy, and cyanoacrylate adhesive (CA).

works well for larger surfaces and irregular joints that don't mate perfectly. Setting time is generally 15 to 30 seconds, making it slow for general-purpose work. Thick CAs include Hot Stuff Super T, Slow Jet, and Zap-A-Gap.

You can cure cyanoacrylate instantly by spraying it with a CA accelerator, such as Insta Set, Jet Set, or Zip Kicker. This is especially handy when using thick CA to fill a large gap. Once the pieces and glue are in place, spraying accelerator will cure the CA. Avoid using accelerator on painted surfaces (it will stain or damage some paints).

Because cyanoacrylate has a fairly short shelf life (about three months after the bottle is opened), don't buy any more than you plan to use in that time. If CA begins to get stringy, or if it begins taking noticeably longer to cure, discard it and buy a new bottle.

Safety

Safety with tools—even simple hand tools—can't be overstressed. Wear safety glasses whenever you're cutting or drilling materials. Small drill bits break readily and can easily fly into an eye. Ditto for the fragile tips of hobby knife blades. Be aware that material being cut, especially when being chopped by a hobby knife, can also easily fly into an eye.

Wear safety glasses at all times when using a motor tool or any other power saw or tool.

Keep fingers out of the way when cutting material with a knife. Position your free hand so that it is away from the intended path of the blade. This will keep your hand out of harm's way when the blade slips (as one eventually will). It's always a good idea, especially with large material, to clamp the material down before cutting.

Wear a dust mask when grinding, sanding, or doing any activity that causes dust. Stray sawdust and other fine particulates can irritate the lungs, nose, and throat.

It's also a good idea to wear hearing protection devices when using loud power tools, especially saws and shop vacuums.

Provide adequate ventilation whenever you're using solvent cements, cyanoacrylate, or solvent-based paint. If you are sensitive to these vapors, wear a NIOSH-approved chemical cartridge respirator to block out vapors.

Since CA will readily bond with skin, keep a bottle of CA debonder (or acetone) handy in case you glue your fingers together (or to a model).

Epoxy can be used in many situations where more glue is required than is practical for CA. Epoxy comes in two parts (epoxy and hardener) that must be mixed together. To use it, squeeze equal parts onto a piece of scrap card or plastic. Mix them together thoroughly with a toothpick. Epoxy is handy for securing weights inside freight cars and reinforcing joints already glued with cyanoacrylate.

White glue is usually the best choice for wood-to-wood joints. It also works well for gluing plaster, paper, cardstock, and other porous materials. It dries clear, but if you're planning to stain wood (such as for trestles), be sure to stain it before gluing—any stray white glue (or CA) on the surface will seal the wood and keep the stain from penetrating.

Yellow carpenter's glue (aliphatic resin) is stronger than white glue, but dries hard and with a yellow tinge. Unless you need additional strength, stick with white glue for most modeling purposes.

Rubber cement is handy for gluing paper items such as signs. If you want a permanent bond, brush a thin coat on both surfaces. Allow the cement to dry to the touch (at least five minutes), then press the surfaces together.

For a temporary, removable bond, brush a thin coat of rubber cement on one surface only. Press the item in place while the cement is still wet.

Now let's move on and find out how to use these tools and materials to improve our models.

chapter three

Couplers

Smooth operation of cars and locomotives depends on couplers that are installed properly and operate flawlessly. We'll start by examining the types of couplers that are available, then show how to choose, install, and maintain them for trouble-free operation.

Horn-hook couplers

Prior to the late 1990s, almost all HO locomotives and rolling stock came equipped with horn-hook couplers (see fig. 3-1). They still are standard on some equipment today. The early popularity of horn-hooks among manufacturers was largely because the design could be used free of charge by any manufacturer.

Although horn-hook couplers are cheap to make and use, they have operational drawbacks. They couple together very easily, but uncoupling is difficult to do by hand and downright impossible remotely. Also, especially if the couplers are truck-mounted, their design makes them exert sideways pressure when pushing cars (as when switching), which sometimes causes cars to derail.

Horn-hook couplers are also ugly. They bear little resemblance to real couplers, and their use detracts from the appearance of otherwise sharp-looking models.

Automatic knuckle couplers

To avoid the problems of horn-hooks, most experienced modelers install automatic knuckle couplers on cars and locomotives.

Kadee's line of Magne-Matic automatic knuckle couplers, developed in the 1950s, has been the de facto standard coupler in the hobby for decades. They look like prototype knuckle couplers, and they operate well. See fig. 3-2.

Fig. 3-1. Horn-hook couplers were once the industry standard, and they still come as standard equipment on some new cars.

In the mid-1990s other companies began offering similar couplers. These include Accurail Accumate (fig. 3-3), Bachmann E-Z Mate, McHenry (fig. 3-4), and Proto 2000 (fig. 3-5). Each differs slightly in design, but all operate in the same way as Kadee couplers and will mate with them.

Fig. 3-2. Kadee's Magne-Matic line of metal knuckle couplers has long been the most popular choice for upgrading rolling stock.

Fig. 3-3. Accurail's Accumate is a two-piece coupler molded in acetal plastic, with a separate steel uncoupling pin (omitted in this view).

Fig. 3-4. The McHenry coupler, molded in acetal plastic, has a built-in spring on the rear of its shank.

Fig. 3-5. Life-Like's Proto 2000 coupler is molded in plastic, with built-in springs on the side of the shank.

With automatic knuckle couplers, coupling is a simple matter of pushing cars together. The metal pin under the coupler remotely uncouples through the use of an undertrack or between-the-rails magnet (see fig. 3-6). You can use the permanent under-track magnets on spurs, but placing them on main lines can cause occasional unwanted uncoupling. Stick to the movable above-tie magnets for these locations, setting them in place as needed.

As long as there's tension on the coupler (as when a train is being pulled), it will stay coupled. To uncouple automatically, position the couplers directly over the magnet, as in fig. 3-7. The magnet will begin pulling the pins apart. Back up slightly, and as the slack is relieved, the knuckles will open wide. The couplers are now apart, as fig. 3-8 shows.

You can now either leave the uncoupled car in place,

Fig. 3-6. Magnets can be mounted permanently under the track, or you can set between-the-rails magnets in place as you need them.

Fig. 3-7. Position the couplers over the magnet, and it will begin pulling the knuckles apart.

Fig. 3-8. As the slack is relieved, the knuckles will open wide.

Fig. 3-9. The cars can now be brought back together, and the uncoupled car can be pushed as far as needed to position it.

Fig. 3-10. Pull the train away from the uncoupled car and the couplers will return to normal position.

Fig. 3-11. Cars can be uncoupled using a small screwdriver or a tool such as the Accurail Switchman.

or—through what Kadee calls the "delayed-action" feature—push it farther down the track. To do this, push the car back toward the uncoupled car. The couplers will meet, but won't couple, as fig. 3-9 shows. The car can then be shoved any distance. Stop beyond the ramp, reverse the direction, and the couplers will return to normal, as in fig. 3-10.

Knuckle couplers can be uncoupled manually by placing a small screwdriver between the knuckles or by using a tool specific for the job, such as the Accurail Switchman, as in fig. 3-11. Slip the tool in place and gently twist, and the knuckles will part.

I strongly urge you to use knuckle couplers for three main reasons. First, most model railroad equipment already comes with them. Second, they operate much better than horn-hooks. Third, they look much, much better.

Also, by choosing knuckle couplers from the beginning you won't be left with a large investment to make when you eventually decide to go with knuckle couplers. You won't regret your choice.

Avoid couplers that use molded plastic knuckle springs—if they're held open long enough, the springs will lose their spring action. Stick to couplers with metal knuckle springs, or those that use the shank springs to close the knuckles (such as the Accumate)

Fine-tuning

For couplers to operate well, they must be installed properly. Important factors include making sure couplers are all installed at the same height, making sure couplers don't droop or sag, and making sure all parts operate smoothly without sticking.

The most important tool in checking and installing couplers is a Kadee coupler height gauge (no. 205), which can be purchased at most hobby shops. Use it to check the couplers on all of your cars and locomotives before placing them in operation.

Figure 3-12 shows how to check a coupler's height. Place the gauge on the track. Roll a car to the gauge. The top of the car's coupler should be even with the top of the coupler on the gauge, and the uncoupling pin should just clear the flat plate at the bottom of the gauge.

(Note: Be sure track power is off when doing this—the coupler gauge is made of metal and will cause a short circuit if there's power to the track.)

Figure 3-13 shows a Proto 2000 flatcar with a low coupler, which is probably the most common problem you'll find. This can be corrected in two ways. The first is to add thin shim washers between the bolster and truck, as fig. 3-14 shows.

This isn't ideal. Although it will correct the coupler height, doing so can make the car itself unprototypically tall. Because of this, only

Fig. 3-12. Couplers should match the Kadee height gauge, and the uncoupling pin should just clear the bottom plate on the gauge.

Fig. 3-13. The most common coupler problem is low placement, as on this Proto 2000 flatcar.

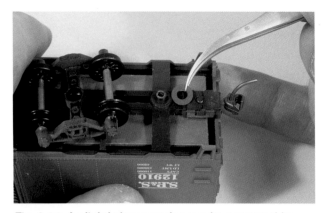

Fig. 3-14. A slightly low coupler can be corrected by adding a thin shim washer between the car bolster and truck, as on this Athearn boxcar.

Fig. 3-15. Substituting a Kadee coupler for an underset shank corrected the height on this flatcar.

Fig. 3-16. Special pliers for adjusting uncoupling pins are made by Kadee and Micro-Mark, but standard pliers can also be used.

use washers for minor adjustments, and don't use multiple washers. Kadee makes fiber washers in .010˝ and .015˝ thicknesses.

The other solution is to use a coupler with an offset coupler shank, as in fig. 3-15. Kadee and McHenry both make couplers with shanks both overset and underset, allowing adjustments regardless of whether the coupler is high or low. The replacement coupler (Kadee no. 28) works perfectly on this flatcar, making it match the gauge.

If the uncoupling pin is too high or too low, bend it in the appropriate direction. You can use a standard pair of pliers for this, but an easier solution is to use special trip-pin pliers, as fig. 3-16 shows. These are available from Kadee, Micro-Mark, and others. Using them in one direction allows you to bend the pin down; flipping the pliers will bend the pin up.

It's critical that the coupler shank move freely from side to side. If it binds, loosen the coupler box screw until the coupler moves freely. Never use oil to lubricate couplers—the oil will collect dirt and impede operations. If necessary, use lubricating powder such as Kadee's powdered graphite to keep parts moving smoothly.

Installing couplers

Most coupler boxes on freight cars today are designed to accept Kadee no. 5 and similar couplers. Simply add the spring and coupler and screw or press the coupler box cover in place. See fig. 3-17.

Many cars have friction pins instead of screws to hold coupler

Replacing springs

The tiny bronze springs that hold the knuckle in place on Kadee and other couplers tend to pop loose, and at first the prospect of replacing one can be daunting.

However, the photo shows an easy method: Grab the spring with a hobby knife blade, which is just thick enough to fit between the coils. Set it on one mounting peg, then compress the spring until it fits onto the second mounting peg and remove the blade.

box covers in place. To increase reliability and reduce the chance that a cover will fall out while a train is running, many modelers replace the pins with screws.

To do coupler installations using 2-56 screws, you'll need a pin vise with nos. 50 and 43 bits and a 2-56 tap. Use the no. 50 bit for drilling screw mounting holes, and use the no. 43 bit any time you need a hole that must clear the mounting screw (such as a coupler box cover). Tapping the mounting hole (cutting the threads in the sides of the hole) ensures that you'll be able to turn the screw into place easily.

This is a simple process. Figure 3-17 shows how to do it on an Accurail car, but the process is the same on other cars. Start by trimming off the friction pin on the cover. Use the mark from the pin as a guide for drilling a no. 43 (clearance) hole. Use a no. 50 bit to enlarge the existing hole on the car (if necessary).

Make threads for the mounting screw by tapping the hole 2-56, as fig. 3-18 shows. Put the tap in a pin vise and slowly turn it into the hole. Pull it out periodically to clear the plastic remnants, then turn it back into the hole.

Fig. 3-17. A new coupler and spring can be simply dropped in place in the built-in coupler boxes on most cars. For increased reliability, friction pins can be replaced with screws, as on this Accurail boxcar.

Fig. 3-18. Use a 2-56 tap to make threads for adding the mounting screw.

Assemble the coupler and spring in the box, put the cover in place, then turn a 2-56 screw into place. By working in assembly line fashion, it's possible to deal with many cars at once.

If the car's coupler box won't readily accept knuckle couplers—or if the car had truck-mounted couplers—mount the coupler on the car in its own box. Use the lid of the coupler box as a guide for marking the location of the screw mounting hole. Make sure that the box is centered on the car. Drill a no. 50 mounting hole, then tap it 2-56. See fig. 3-19.

Cut off the side mounting "wings" on the Kadee coupler box, as in fig. 3-20. Assemble the coupler and spring inside the box, then screw the box to the car, as in fig. 3-21. Place the car on the tracks, check the coupler against the Kadee coupler height gauge, and make any adjustments necessary.

Fig. 3-19. To body-mount a coupler to a car, use the lid of the coupler box cover to mark the hole location, then drill a no. 50 hole and tap it 2-56.

Fig. 3-20. Cut off the side mounting pods on the Kadee coupler box before mounting it.

Fig. 3-21. Screw the new coupler and box into place.

Sagging coupler

At first glance, the coupler on the Athearn car appears to be too low. However, if you look closely, you can see that the coupler is sagging downward. A look at the end of the car reveals the problem: The vertical gap in the coupler box is deeper than the thickness of the coupler shank. The result is that the coupler flops vertically, which will cause poor operations, including unwanted uncoupling.

You can solve the problem two ways: by substituting a coupler with a thicker shank, or by gluing a thin piece of styrene plastic into the box. In this case, gluing the shim to the bottom of the box made the coupler come out at the correct height. Styrene is available in many thicknesses, but .005″ and .010″ are the handiest for shimming coupler boxes.

Fig. 3-22. Make a coupler mounting pad behind the pilot with layers of styrene, then drill a mounting hole, tap it, and add the new coupler in its box.

Couplers on locomotives

Mounting knuckle couplers on locomotives has become much easier in recent years—most now either come with knuckle couplers or have boxes or openings that accept them.

However, if you're working on older Athearn and other locomotives, you'll discover that mounting knuckle couplers requires some creativity. The keys are to make sure that the coupler box is connected solidly to either the frame or the shell, and that the coupler comes out level and at the proper height.

Because of potential clearance problems, it's wise to use couplers with mounting boxes smaller than the standard Kadee no. 5. Good choices are the Kadee no. 8 or any of the couplers in Kadee's 30-series.

On older Athearn diesels—and many other locomotives of the same basic design—the best method generally is to use a hacksaw to cut off the old coupler mounting arm on the cast-metal frame, then mount a new coupler to the shell.

Build up a new coupler mounting pad by gluing layers of styrene behind the pilot, as fig. 3-22 shows. Check to make sure the height will be correct. Drill a mounting hole in the pad, tap it for a 2-56 screw, and install the coupler in its box.

Be strict in testing couplers, and don't let any cars on your layout with couplers that aren't working properly. The reward will be reliable operation.

chapter four

Wheels and Trucks

Along with track, wheels are vital to the smooth operation of rolling

stock. Each wheel has a flange on the inside that keeps it on the rail.

The axle connects two wheels back to back, and the combination of an

axle and two wheels is called a wheelset.

The truck is the frame that holds the wheelsets. Most freight car trucks have four wheels; some passenger trucks and heavy-duty freight trucks have six wheels. Figure 4-1 shows the parts of wheelsets and trucks.

Wheelsets

Model wheelsets can be cast in engineering plastic as a single piece, or they can have plastic or metal wheels on separate plastic, steel, or brass axles. It is vital that wheelsets, like couplers, be checked to ensure smooth operation. For this you'll need a National Model Railroad Association standards gauge, as shown in fig. 4-2.

The most important factor is that each wheelset be in gauge. Figure 4-2 shows a cast-plastic wheelset from a train set car shown in Chapter 1. Note how the wheelset is narrow in gauge—the flanges should rest in the notches on the gauge.

The notches also mark the proper depth of a flange to match the NMRA's RP25 wheel contour. The wheels shown have flanges much deeper than the standard. Contrary to what many beginners think, deep flanges won't help wheels stay on the rails better than RP25 flanges. Deep flanges can bump track spikes or bottom out in grade crossings and turnouts. Flanges whose angle is too sharp can "pick" turnout points, resulting in derailments.

Figure 4-3 shows a wheelset from Athearn. Note that it is in gauge and that the flanges are the proper depth. There's nothing you can do to fix a bad single-piece wheelset like the one in fig. 4-2—just throw it out and substitute a new one.

Wheel sizes

Several wheel sizes are available, so it's important to know which wheels are correct for each type of car. Wheel measurements are always in diameter, measured across the wheel tread. The most common sizes are 33″ and 36″, but 38″ and 28″ are also used sometimes.

Use 33″ wheels on all freight cars with 70-ton capacity and less. This includes most freight cars built before the early 1960s, as well as most modern boxcars, refrigerator cars, gondolas, and flatcars. Check the capacity line ("CAPY") line in the car's data, and if it's 140,000 pounds or less, use 33″ wheels.

Use 36″ wheels on passenger cars and all freight cars of 100-ton capacity (up to 210,000 pounds in the CAPY line). These include jumbo covered hoppers, most modern tank cars, and modern coal hoppers and coal gondolas.

Equipment of 125-ton capacity or more must use 38″ wheelsets. This currently includes some articulated well-style intermodal cars.

Triple-deck autorack cars (which are 70-ton cars) may use low-profile 28″ wheels for clearance purposes.

Fig. 4-1. Wheelset and truck parts

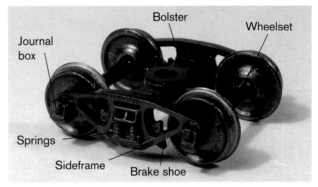

Fig. 4-2. The flanges should rest in the notches on the NMRA gauge. This wheelset is narrow in gauge, and the flanges are deeper than NMRA recommends.

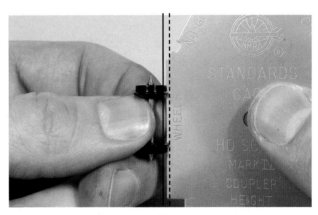

Fig. 4-3. This Athearn wheelset is in gauge, with flanges at the proper depth.

Wheelsets with separate wheels and axles, such as the Athearn one in fig. 4-3, can be fixed if they are out of gauge. Figure 4-4 shows how to twist a wheel in or out with your fingers. (If the wheels are stubborn, you might have to grab the axle with pliers.)

When adjusting wheelsets, be sure that the wheels are properly centered on the axle as well as being in gauge. Once the wheel is in gauge, add a drop of cyanoacrylate adhesive (CA) inside the wheel at the axle to hold it in place.

Most experienced modelers favor metal wheels over plastic ones. Metal wheels add weight to a car down low, thus lowering the car's center of gravity. They tend to polish themselves against the track, keeping them (and the track) cleaner. Plastic wheels tend to accumulate dirt over time.

Metal wheels also look better. Most metal wheels have more accurate profiles than plastic ones, and the shiny metal treads look much more realistic than their plastic counterparts.

Most high-quality replacement wheelsets have metal wheels. These include wheelsets from InterMountain, Kadee, Life-Like Proto 2000, NorthWest Short Line, and Reboxx.

Wheels with the NMRA-recommended width (a .110″ tire width, which includes the flange and tread) operate very well, but the wheels are quite a bit wider in scale than the real thing.

Because of this, some manufacturers now offer wheels in "semi-scale" versions, such as the InterMountain wheelset in fig. 4-5. They have a visibly narrower profile than standard wheels (.088″ tire width), but they still operate well on most commercial track components.

Be aware that on broad turnouts (above no. 6) or on turnouts with wider-than-standard flangeways, these wheels can fall into the flangeways and possibly derail. If in doubt, run a test car through your trackwork before changing the wheelsets on all of your equipment.

On the extreme end of wheel size are scale wheels, which have dimensions matching prototype standards. The NorthWest Short Line wheelset in fig. 4-5 is one example. Note the thin profile and shallow flange. They are favored among modelers building display models and those building track to fine scale or Proto:87 standards. They will drop into flangeway gaps in many commer-

Polishing wheel treads

Many wheelsets (notably Kadee) have been chemically blackened. Their treads can be polished with a wire brush in a motor tool, as the photo shows. Use a low speed on the motor tool, and hold the other wheel on the axle loosely to keep it rotating slowly. Excess speed can heat the plastic parts, causing them to melt.

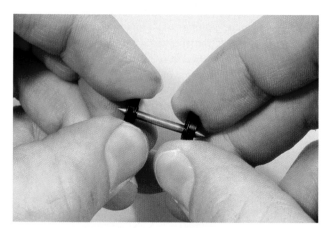

Fig. 4-4. If a three-piece wheelset is out of gauge, twist a wheel on the axle until the wheelset is in gauge.

Fig. 4-5. Replacement metal wheels include (from top) scale wheelsets from NorthWest Short Line, semi-scale wheels from InterMountain, and standard wheels from Kadee.

cial turnouts, making them impractical for use on many layouts.

Replacing a wheelset is easy. Just pull the truck frame apart slightly while slipping the new wheelset in place.

Trucks

The trucks on most model cars are single-piece castings made from acetal plastic, a slippery engineering plastic (Delrin is one name brand). This material is self-lubricating, making it ideal for friction points such as needle-point axles inside a truck sideframe.

Some trucks—notably those made by Kadee—are metal. Kadee's trucks include actual springs (they are simply molded plastic in others), and the bolster can actually ride up and down on the springs. These are known as equalized trucks. See fig. 4-6. Both styles of trucks will operate well.

Model trucks are based on prototype trucks that fall into one of two categories: solid-bearing (sometimes incorrectly called friction-bearing) and roller-bearing.

Until the 1960s most real freight cars used solid-bearing trucks, as shown in fig. 4-1. The journal boxes on these trucks held packing material impregnated in oil to lubricate the axle end and bearing. They required frequent lubrication, making them an operational headache.

Roller-bearing trucks were used on some equipment starting in the 1940s, and they became mandatory on all new prototype cars in the late 1960s. These trucks require little maintenance and have sealed roller bearings in place of journal boxes. See fig. 4-7.

Trucks are secured to model cars in one of two ways: snap-fit (fig. 4-8) or by means of a screw or friction pin. Most train-set-quality cars have snap-on trucks; higher-quality cars have trucks screwed in place.

Replacing a pair of trucks is usually a simple matter of unscrewing the old truck, replacing the truck, and replacing the screw.

To upgrade a car whose original truck was the snap-in-place variety, you'll need to fill the original mounting hole and drill a new one, as fig. 4-9 shows. I suggest making a plug from 1/8" plastic tubing, gluing it in place, then drilling it with a no. 50 bit and tapping the hole for a 2-56 screw. You can also fill the hole with modeling putty, let it harden, and drill a new mounting hole.

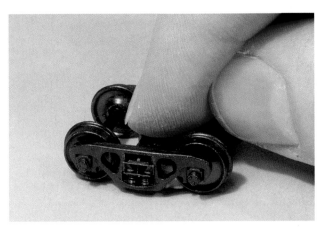

Fig. 4-6. Kadee's trucks are metal, with bolsters that move on their springs much like real trucks.

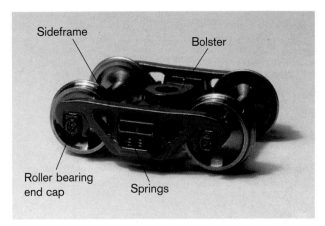

Fig. 4-7. This Athearn truck has roller-bearing end caps that rotate, just like the real thing.

Fig. 4-8. Most train set cars have trucks that snap into place on the body.

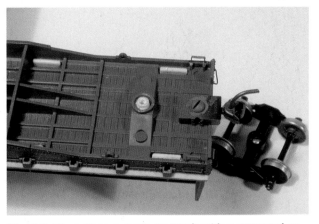

Fig. 4-9. To replace a snap-on truck with a screwed-on truck, glue a piece of 1/8" styrene tubing in the hole, drill out the hole with a no. 50 bit, and tap it 2-56.

Fine-tuning

Cars should roll smoothly down the track without rocking or wobbling. If a car wobbles, first make sure that there are no stray bits of flash or plastic where the car bolster and truck meet. See fig. 4-10. If these surfaces aren't flat, the car will lean or wobble.

Turn one truck-mounting screw until the truck is firmly against the car. See fig. 4-11. Then unscrew it slowly, just far enough to allow the truck to turn freely. Leave the second truck fairly loose. Set the car on the track and test it for wobble. If it still wobbles, turn the second screw in until the wobble disappears.

If a car doesn't roll freely, chances are that the trucks are binding with the needle-point ends of the axles. Don't use oil to lubricate axles and bearings on trucks: The oil will only pick up dust and dirt, further impairing operation.

Instead, get rid of the material that's causing the binding. You can sometimes do this with a hobby knife, but the tool shown in fig. 4-12 (the no. 82838-3111 Truck Tuner from Micro-Mark) is designed for reaming the bearing points of a truck. (Drill bits won't work well for this because of their cutting angle.) Set the tool in place and turn it a few times to clean the bearings.

It's important to keep wheels clean. This is especially true of plastic ones, which tend to build up more grime than metal ones. Do this in the same way as you clean locomotive wheels (see Chapter 5), by placing a paper towel across the tracks and wetting it with track cleaner or Goo Gone. Roll each truck of each car back and forth across the towel until the wheels are clean.

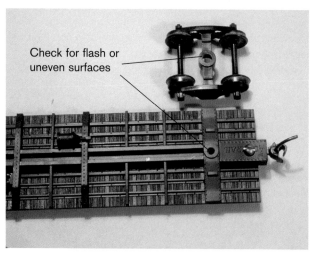

Fig. 4-10. Check the bearing surfaces on the truck and body for flash or stray material.

Fig. 4-11. To eliminate wobbling, turn one screw until the truck is tight, then unscrew it just until the truck swivels freely. Leave the other truck fairly loose.

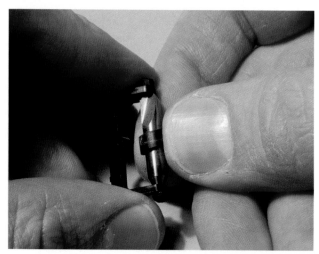

Fig. 4-12. The Truck Tuner tool from Micro-Mark reams sticky truck bearings at the proper angle, helping wheelsets to roll freely.

chapter five

Maintaining Locomotives

Smooth-running locomotives make it a joy to run trains, while a balky engine that runs erratically or stalls frequently will quickly cause you to feel frustration and can even make you lose interest in the hobby. Here, we'll look at what it takes to get model engines running well and keep them in good shape.

Chapter 1 described some properties to look for in model locomotives. Look for locomotives whose axles are all powered (all drivers for steam locomotives). They should pick up electricity from all wheels. The more electrical contact points a locomotive has, the better it will fight its way through dirty track.

When you buy a locomotive, you generally get what you pay for. Inexpensive train-set quality engines are fine for pulling small trains around in circles, but you'll find they aren't as powerful as good-quality scale models. Rarely do they perform as well, run as smoothly and quietly, or last as long.

High-quality diesels are made by Athearn, Atlas, Bachmann Spectrum, InterMountain, Kato, Life-Like (Proto 1000 and Proto 2000), Stewart, and Walthers Trainline. Solid steam locomotives are made by Athearn, Bachmann Spectrum, Proto 2000, IHC, Rivarossi, and Trix.

Diesel locomotives

Most newer locomotive models are virtually maintenance-free. They run well, and the only maintenance necessary is periodic lubrication. However, every once in a while you'll need to troubleshoot a locomotive or fix something that requires some disassembly.

Manufacturers use a variety of methods to attach the shell to the frame/chassis. Some use tabs on the shell; others use screws driven up from under the frame. Check the instructions or assembly diagram before attempting to remove a shell.

Once you get inside, you'll find that most diesels are built in similar fashion. Figure 5-1 shows a Proto 2000 GP9. Electrical connections on this and most other newer models are routed through

Fig. 5-1. This Proto 2000 GP9 shows typical diesel model construction. Lifting off the injection-molded styrene shell reveals weights covering the engine and mechanism and all wiring routed through a circuit board mounted at the top.

printed-circuit boards located atop the frame. This makes it easier to add a Digital Command Control decoder, as the chapter on wiring will explain. It also makes it easier to replace headlight bulbs.

On locomotives like this one the weights must be removed to gain access to the motor and drive mechanism. Other locomotives have connections hard-wired, or have metal strips that slide against each other.

Most diesel models have a motor at the middle of the frame with a flywheel at one or both ends. Figure 5-2 shows the motor and mechanism. This one is an Athearn model, and its brushes and commutator are exposed; other models have enclosed motors.

The motor is connected to each truck tower using a universal

Fig. 5-2. Athearn motor and mechanism with exposed brushes and commutator.

Fig. 5-3. Removing the cover atop the truck tower provides access to the worm and top of the truck gears.

Fig. 5-4. Removing the cover plate reveals the truck and axle gears.

joint. This driveshaft turns a worm at the top of each truck tower, and a series of gears transfers motion from the worm to the axles. Figure 5-3 shows the cover removed from the Athearn gear tower to gain access to the worm.

Gaining access to the truck gears is sometimes a matter of removing a cover plate, as in fig. 5-4, although on some locomotives this requires disassembling the trucks.

The figures on the previous page show the key points for lubrication. Check these spots every couple of months (or 20 hours or so of operation). Apply lubrication sparingly—a little goes a long way, and most gears are made of engineering plastic, which requires very little lubrication.

Use a plastic-compatible light oil such as LaBelle no. 108 on the motor, axle, and worm bearings. On truck gears use a plastic-compatible light grease such as LaBelle no. 106. Simply apply a drop or dab of lubricant to one of the gears, and operation will distribute it evenly.

Many new locomotives are grossly overlubricated at the factory. Check for this, and use the corner of a soft cloth to wipe up any excess oil or grease from the lubrication points.

If an engine runs noisily or erratically, make sure that the worm and all gears are seated firmly in place and that all covers are firmly snapped in place. Check the universal joint and all gears for stray molding flash, and make sure there's no foreign material (carpet fibers, dirt, etc.) in the truck gear enclosure.

On engines with exposed commutator and brushes (such as in fig. 5-2), make sure the commutator is clean. You can use a pencil eraser to polish this area while turning the driveshaft by hand. Make sure no stray material gets into the motor.

Fig. 5-5. This International Hobby Corp. 2-8-0 has an injection-molded styrene shell that is attached to the frame by means of a screw and plastic tabs.

Steam locomotives

Figure 5-5 shows an International Hobby Corp. 2-8-0. It has a typical arrangement for a model steam locomotive drive, as fig. 5-6 shows. The motor is usually in the cab (or in the firebox or boiler near the cab), with the driveshaft and worm powering one of the driver axles near the cab. Gain access by removing the boiler/cab shell from the chassis. Check the instructions before doing this to see how the boiler and chassis are attached.

Figure 5-7 shows the same locomotive from the bottom. The cover plate under the drivers has been removed. On most steam locomotive models, such as this one, the geared driver set powers the remaining drivers via the locomotive's side rods.

As you would on a diesel, use a light oil on the driver bearings and a light grease in the gears.

Fig. 5-6. Removing the shell shows the motor (with a small flywheel that protrudes into the cab) and worm, which drives a gear on the third set of drivers.

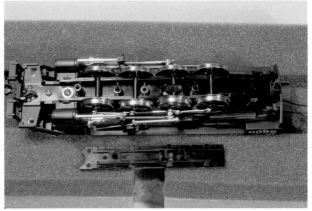

Fig. 5-7. Removing the bottom plate provides access to the axle bearings as well as the driver gear.

Cleaning wheels

If a locomotive begins to run erratically, nine times out of ten the cause is dirty wheels. Figure 5-8 shows an easy way to clean locomotive wheels. Place a paper towel damp with cleaning fluid (such as Goo Gone, a liquid track cleaner) on a scrap piece of track.

Clip wires from a power pack to the track, and run a locomotive onto the paper towel so only one truck (or half the drivers) is on the towel. Turn up the throttle and let the wheels turn themselves clean. Turn the locomotive around and clean the remaining wheels.

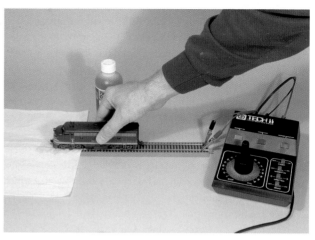

Fig. 5-8. Place cleaning fluid on a paper towel across the tracks. Running the engine over the towel cleans the wheels quite effectively.

Steam locomotive wheel arrangements

Steam locomotives are known by their wheel arrangements following the Whyte classification system. To use it, count the total number of wheels on the lead truck, followed by the number of drivers, followed by the number of wheels on the trailing truck. In addition, many steam locomotive types have nicknames by which they are known.

This chart lists the most common steam locomotive types, although many other wheel arrangements were used. Also included are their nicknames and most common uses.

Arrangement	Side view	Nickname	Use
0-4-0	< OO		Switching (early)
0-6-0	< OOO		Switching
0-8-0	< OOOO		Switching (modern)
2-6-0	< oOOO	Mogul	Freight (early)
2-8-0	< oOOOO	Consolidation	Freight
2-10-0	< oOOOOO	Decapod	Freight
2-6-2	< oOOOo	Prairie	Freight (early)
2-8-2	< oOOOOo	Mikado	Freight
2-10-2	< oOOOOOo	Santa Fe	Freight
2-8-4	< oOOOOoo	Berkshire	Fast freight (modern)
2-10-4	< oOOOOOoo	Texas	Heavy freight
4-4-0	< ooOO	American	Passenger (early)
4-6-0	< ooOOO	Ten-Wheeler	Passenger, freight (early)
4-4-2	< ooOOo	Atlantic	Fast passenger (early)
4-6-2	< ooOOOo	Pacific	Passenger
4-8-2	< ooOOOOo	Mountain	Heavy passenger
4-6-4	< ooOOOoo	Hudson	Fast passenger
4-8-4	< ooOOOOoo	Northern	Passenger, fast freight (modern)
2-8-8-2	< o OOOO OOOO o	Mallet	Freight
4-6-6-4	< oo OOO OOO oo	Challenger	Passenger, fast freight (modern)
4-8-8-4	< oo OOOO OOOO oo	Big Boy	Freight (modern)

chapter six

Building and Upgrading Freight Cars

Chapter 1 looked at many of the characteristics that distinguish a high-quality car from a train-set model, including separate ladders, grab irons, brake gear, and other details; metal wheels; body-mounted knuckle couplers; and realistic paint schemes. In the past, a modeler had to assemble a kit to get fine detail.

That's no longer true, as today many high-quality freight cars are available ready-to-run, including those from Athearn, Atlas, InterMountain, Kadee, Life-Like Proto 1000 and Proto 2000, Walthers, and others.

There are still many fine kits on the market, and they range from easy-to-assemble cars to craftsman-level kits in plastic and resin. Good plastic kits are available from Accurail, Athearn, Bowser, Branchline, Model Die Casting, InterMountain, Red Caboose, and Walthers, among others.

Simple kit

If you've never built a kit before, a good place to start is with a simple freight car. The photos show the steps in building a two-bay hopper car from Accurail. It's a typical easy-to-assemble kit with good, realistic detail and paint scheme, but with simplified detailing, including molded-on grab irons and brake gear without piping. The assembly steps will be similar for other basic cars.

Figure 6-1 shows what you get when you open the box. Start by scanning the instruction sheet. Then cut parts from the sprues as necessary with a flush sprue cutter or a hobby knife. Remove

any superfluous mold flash or sprue remains, as fig. 6-2 shows.

On most freight cars the weight is concealed in the car, but on some hoppers (including this one) the weights are exposed (they represent the hopper end sheets). Paint them to match the car color—in this case black. See fig. 6-3.

Brake components will usually have plastic pins molded in place to match holes on the frame or underbody. Be sure not to cut these pins off when removing them from the sprue. See fig. 6-4. Add the brake parts, gluing them in place with liquid plastic cement, as in fig. 6-5.

Test-fit the frame to the body, making sure it will fit securely. Use a hobby knife to scrape the paint away from areas on the body where the frame will be glued. See fig. 6-6.

Set the weights in place, then use the needle-point applicator on the thick plastic cement bottle to run a thin bead of cement under the body where the frame will go. Press the frame firmly in place (it will hold the weights securely in position). Make sure the frame is held in place snugly while the glue dries. You have to use your imagination for some cars—fig. 6-7 shows how I did it on the hopper car.

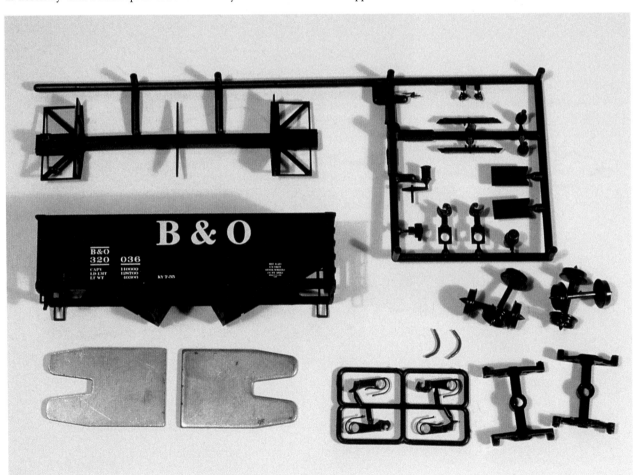

Fig. 6-1. Here's what you get with a simple freight car kit—in this case, an Accurail hopper car.

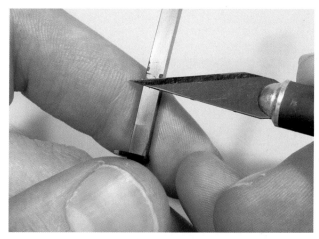

Fig. 6-2. After cutting parts from their sprues, use a hobby knife to shave off any sprue remnants.

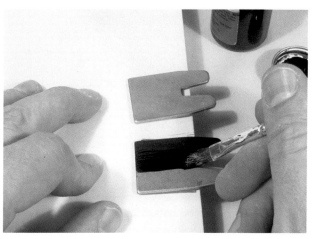

Fig. 6-3. On some hopper cars the weights are exposed. Paint them to match the car—in this case, black.

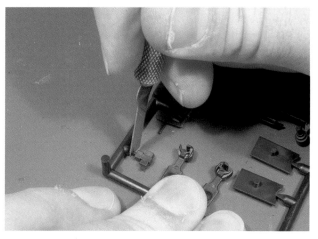

Fig. 6-4. When cutting parts from their sprues, be careful not to confuse mounting pins with sprue gates.

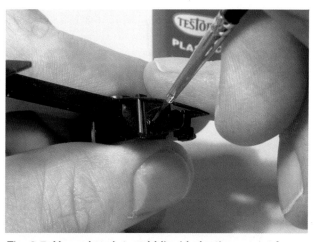

Fig. 6-5. Use a brush to add liquid plastic cement from behind the mounting hole.

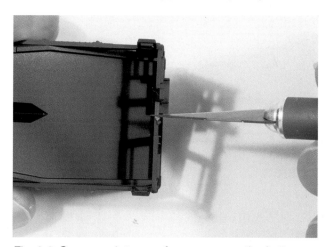

Fig. 6-6. Scrape paint away from areas on the bottom of the body where the frame will be glued in place.

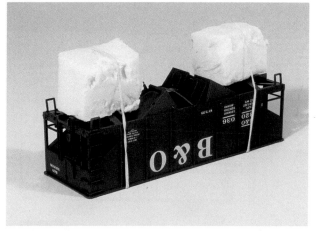

Fig. 6-7. Rubber bands work well to hold the frame to the body on most cars, but spacers such as these blocks of foam are sometimes necessary.

Fig. 6-8. Add remaining details by placing small drops of glue on the body with a toothpick, then pressing the parts into place.

Fig. 6-9. Here's the completed Accurail hopper car.

Add any remaining details to the car, in this case the brake lever and hopper door latches and details. See fig. 6-8. Use a toothpick to place small drops of plastic cement or cyanoacrylate adhesive (CA) on the car, then use tweezers to carefully set the parts in place.

Add your choice of couplers (see Chapter 3 for more details). Snap the wheelsets into place on the trucks and add the trucks to the car with screws or friction pins. Figure 6-9 shows the completed kit.

Complex plastic kit

Many kits fall into the category of craftsman plastic kits. These include kits from Branchline, InterMountain, Life-Like Proto 2000, Red Caboose, Tichy, and others. Opening the box of one of these can be intimidating (fig. 6-10 shows a Red Caboose boxcar). However, if you've assembled a couple of basic kits, moving up to a craftsman kit is just a matter of taking your time through each construction step.

Let's go through building the Red Caboose boxcar step by step. Start by reading through the instructions and becoming familiar with the parts. Cut the parts from their sprues as you go. It helps you identify the parts if you leave them on the sprues until you need them. Use care when trimming parts, and use a hobby knife to trim any flash.

Assembly varies by car type, but most kits group the assembly

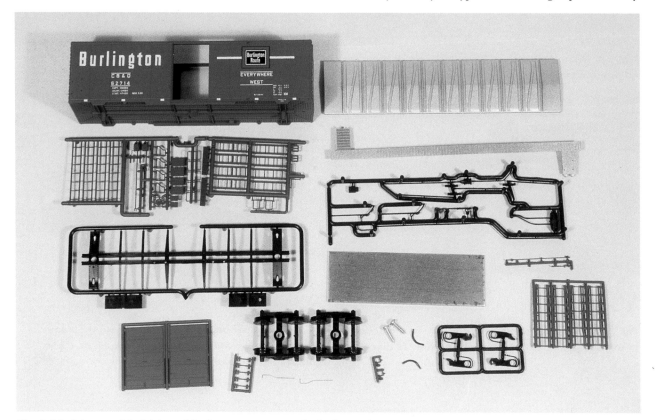

Fig. 6-10. Advanced freight car kits have more parts, including individual grab irons and ladders, detailed brake gear and piping, and separate roofs (and sometimes ends).

Fig. 6-11. Use glue sparingly, as on this running board support.

Fig. 6-12. Flat steel weights are handy for holding parts in place while glue dries, as on this running board/roof subassembly.

steps into subassemblies. For this boxcar, it starts by adding the running board to the roof. Use a hobby knife to scrape the paint from the supports on the roof. Use a toothpick to place liquid plastic cement on each support, as fig. 6-11 shows.

Place the running board in position, taking care to align it properly. With this style of kit, parts sometimes have no locator pins—you have to align things on your own. Flat weights are handy for keeping things in place while glue dries. See fig. 6-12.

Once the roof dries, add the corner grabs to the running board. Figure 6-13 shows one method of gluing separate details with mounting pegs: Put a few drops of medium-viscosity cyanoacry-late on a piece of scrap plastic. Dip just the tips of the mounting

pegs of the part into the CA, then carefully set the part in place.

Move to the next subassembly—in this case, the underframe. Add the train line to the underframe following the instructions, then test-fit the frame to the car. As you did on the Accurail car, scrape the paint from the mating surfaces, then glue the frame in place with CA or thick plastic cement.

Next comes the brake equipment, starting with the control valve and reservoir, followed by the cylinder, rods, and levers. The brake gear, with its piping and rods, is usually the most delicate part of a car kit, so use care when trimming it from the sprue and when fitting it on the car. See fig. 6-14.

Test-fit the gear, then glue it in place, as in fig. 6-15. Glue the

Fig. 6-13. If a detail part has mounting pegs, dip the pegs in cyanoacrylate, then set them in place on the model.

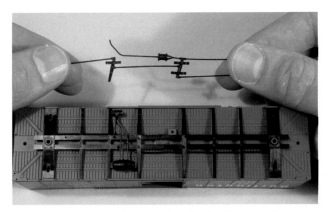

Fig. 6-14. Take care in trimming the brake gear from the sprues. Test-fit everything before gluing it in place.

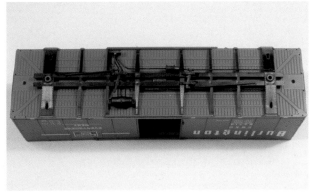

Fig. 6-15. Here's the completed underframe.

ends of the piping into their places on the valve and other locations following the instructions.

Carefully trim the grab irons from their sprues. Use a toothpick to place a small amount of CA in the mounting holes, then set each grab iron in place. Some cars have mounting holes that go through the car body, and you can apply glue from behind.

Installing the brake wheel and related parts often requires drilling a few holes in the end. Some kits have locating dimples on the inside, making it easy to locate holes, but this one does not. Use the parts as guides for marking and then drilling mounting holes (fig. 6-16). Glue the parts in place.

I decided to give the car a different look by modeling one of the doors in a slightly open position. Since part of the interior will be visible, I brush-painted the floor with Polly Scale Grimy Black, as fig. 6-17 shows. The doors can then be glued in place.

Add couplers, as Chapter 3 explains. For this car, drill out the coupler box mounting holes with a no. 50 bit, then tap the hole 2-56 and screw the coupler and box into place. I used a Kadee no. 58 (scale-size) coupler in a Kadee box. Painting the mounting screw black helps hide it from view.

I decided to replace the kit's plastic wheelsets with sets of InterMountain's no. 40052 semi-scale metal wheels. Screw the trucks into place under the car.

The car itself, with its small steel weight, weighed in at three ounces (1.75 ounces without the weight). Since I was modeling with the door open, I didn't want a weight visible inside.

Fig. 6-16. Some cars require mounting holes to be drilled for details on the ends or sides.

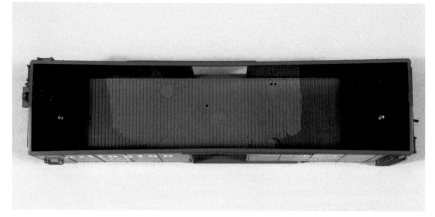

Fig. 6-17. If you're planning to leave the doors open, paint the floor grimy black for a realistic dirty appearance.

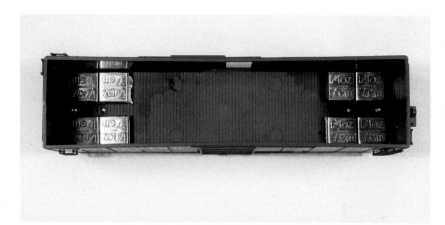

Fig. 6-18. Since the open doors make the middle of the interior visible, weights were added out of sight at each end. Be sure to balance the weights for stability.

Fig. 6-19. Touch up any unpainted areas, or any areas where sprue-removal marks are apparent. An exact paint match isn't necessary.

To solve this, I set aside the car's weight and added two ounces of A-Line peel-and-stick weights (no. 13000), as fig. 6-18 shows. This brought the car's weight up to the NMRA-recommended 3.75 ounces.

Glue the roof in place by running a bead of liquid plastic cement around the inside surface of the top of the sides and ends, then pressing the roof in place.

Cars often have small marks where parts were removed from sprues. Use paint (it doesn't have to be an exact match) to touch up these areas, as well as any unpainted areas, such as the uncoupling levers on this car. See fig. 6-19. Figure 6-20 shows the completed model.

Dressing up freight cars

There are a number of things you can do to improve the looks and operation of your freight cars. Two important things are fine-tuning or upgrading the couplers and wheelsets, as explained in Chapters 3 and 4.

One very realistic addition is weathering. If you look at freight cars in real life, you'll notice that few are clean. Most have a coating of dirt, rust, and grime. Adding this look to your models adds to their realism, making them look as though they've been earning their keep on your railroad.

There are many methods for adding weathering, but chalks are perhaps the easiest way to add many effects. Figure 6-21 shows how I added some grimy effects to the Burlington boxcar. Use a

Fig. 6-20. Here's the completed Red Caboose boxcar. The separate grab irons, underbody brake gear, and other details make it a striking model.

Fig. 6-21. Use a stiff brush to streak powdered chalk onto the model.

Weighting cars

Consistent weighting of your rolling stock is important for reliable operation. Cars that are too light have a tendency to be unstable and are more likely to derail, especially if they are placed in a train ahead of heavier cars.

The National Model Railroad Association (NMRA) has established a recommended practice for weighting cars. The formula for HO scale is an initial weight of one ounce, plus an additional half ounce for each inch of car length.

For example, a 50-foot boxcar in HO scale is about 7 inches long. Using the formula, we can calculate an initial weight of 1 ounce plus .5 ounce per inch (7 x .5 = 3.5) for a total of 4.5 ounces.

Check car weights before assembling kits—once a car is put together, it's difficult to add weight.

The handiest way to add weights is by using the peel-and-stick type, such as the A-Line weights in the Burlington boxcar. A-Line and others also offer lead sheet or lead shot (BBs) that work well in some applications.

Keep the weights centered both side to side and end to end, or the car will tend to lean. Also, keep the weight as low as possible to keep the car's center of gravity low.

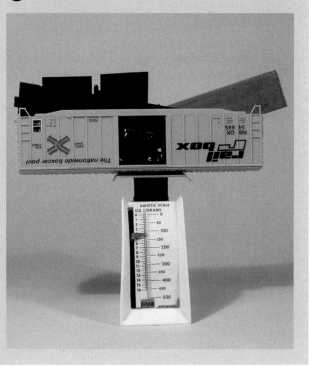

hobby knife to scrape some chalk powder from artist's pastel chalks. Brush the powder onto the model with a stiff brush (hog-bristle brushes are inexpensive and work well).

Use various colors for different effects. Black and dark gray work well for grime and exhaust effects; browns and oranges are good for simulating rust; and white is good for a chalky appearance or for simulating loads such as limestone and powdered cement.

You can seal the chalks with a light clear overspray of clear flat or satin finish. My favorite for this is Model Master Clear Semi-Gloss. Figure 6-22 shows the completed boxcar.

Another way of dressing up model railroading freight cars is to add loads to them. Loads of many types are available from Chooch, Jaeger, Walthers, and others.

Figure 6-23 shows some Chooch coal loads designed to fit the Accurail hopper car shown earlier in the chapter. Adding one of them to the car was a simple matter of removing it from the package and sliding it into place. See fig. 6-24.

Figure 6-25 shows another load from Chooch, this time a scrap metal load for a gondola. For the most realistic effect, paint individual items in the load with various rust and grime colors. Add spacers at each end of the car to raise the load to the proper level (fig. 6-26), then glue the load in place, as fig. 6-27 shows.

Fig. 6-22. The now-grimy car looks as though it has been in service for a while.

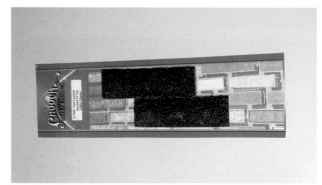

Fig. 6-23. Chooch makes these cast coal loads specifically for the Accurail hopper car.

Fig. 6-24. Adding the load was a simple matter of sliding it in place. The car has also received a coat of chalk weathering.

Fig. 6-25. Painting this gondola load with various rust colors greatly improved its appearance.

Fig. 6-26. Styrene blocks at each end of the Model Die Casting gondola raised the load to the proper height.

Fig. 6-27. Loads can be trimmed to make them fit into variously sized cars.

chapter seven

Benchwork

Although it can be fun to run trains around on the floor, it's best if you can get the trains onto their own table. The table and other support structure for a model railroad are known as benchwork. There are many types of benchwork, but we'll focus on the basics.

Start reading model railroad magazines and books, and you'll quickly notice that many small layouts are designed to fit in a 4 x 8-foot space. This is no coincidence, since that measurement matches the size of a sheet of plywood.

For starters, simply get the track off the floor. The simplest way to do this is to place a sheet of plywood atop a pair of sawhorses. Although not permanent, this will provide a level, solid place for the track while you experiment with track plans and arrange structures and other items. Once you have a track plan picked out and have an idea of what you'd like to do for scenery, you can build something more permanent.

Figure 7-1 shows one way of building a permanent basic table using standard dimensional lumber. For the tabletop choose A/C or B/C (the letters refer to the quality of the finish on each side) plywood with the good side up. Use ½˝ or thicker plywood—thinner plywood will tend to sag.

You can make a simpler and more temporary table by building the 1 x 4 tabletop framework with plywood top as the drawing shows, but placing the top on a pair of sawhorses. Figure 7-2 shows an example.

If you're just getting started, a flat tabletop is just fine. It allows you to play with different track arrangements and position structures and other details without committing to anything.

As you gain experience, you'll notice that varying the elevation of track, roads, and other items is a great way to add scenic interest. You can do this in a couple of ways.

A traditional method that still works well is known as the "cookie-cutter" technique. Figure 7-3 shows the basic idea. With cookie-cutter benchwork, you cut the table along the track, roads, rivers, lakes, and other scenic contours. Placing hidden risers under these areas allows you to raise and lower these elements. The photo on page 41 shows the results of cutting a table in cookie-cutter fashion. Adding scenery hides the openings and edges of the plywood.

Fig. 7-1

Frame sides
1 x 4 x 10˝

Frame ends
and joists,
1 x 4 x 46½˝

Joists on
19˝ centers

Legs, 2 x 4˝

Side brace
omitted for
clarity

Braces, 1 x 2˝
cut to fit

Gussets, ¼˝ plywood

Braces, 1 x 2˝

6˝

Options

There are many ways of approaching benchwork. Some modelers stick to table-style layouts, while others prefer an around-the-walls style, as in fig. 7-4. Running a layout around the walls allows long straightaways and broad curves, both of which are difficult to do on a table. This approach also utilizes space well, because the layout shelf doesn't have to be wide. In fact, 2 feet is fairly wide for a shelf layout. You can easily decrease the width to a foot or even less if you have to get around a tight area.

Some modelers build double-deck layouts to get the most model railroad in a given space. See fig. 7-5. The mechanics of doing this are beyond the reach of this book, but it shows what is possible.

These ideas will get you going, but they don't come close to covering all of the benchwork options open to you. For more details on benchwork, see the book *Basic Model Railroad Benchwork*, published by Kalmbach Publishing Co.

Bill Zuback

Fig. 7-2. *Model Railroader*'s Red Wing project layout was a 4 x 8-foot model railroad. The layout top simply rested on a pair of sawhorses.

Keith Thompson

Fig. 7-4. Jim Chukinas built his HO layout on a 30˝-wide shelf.

Paul Dolkos

Fig. 7-5. This HO layout featuring the Florida East Coast Railway's Key West Extension uses two shelf-style decks around a room to get as much model railroad as possible into the space.

Benchwork tips

- **Use good lumber.** The wood doesn't have to be cabinet grade, but avoid wood with large knots and avoid all lumber that's twisted or bowed. Be picky.
- **Use screws for construction.** Screws hold parts solidly and are easily driven with a cordless drill/driver. Driving nails is a loud process than can loosen earlier nail joints.
- **Don't use particle board or OSB for tabletops.** Particle board is dense, heavy, and difficult to work with; OSB (oriented-stranded board) has a surface that's rough and uneven.
- **Keep grades reasonable.** If you change track elevation, keep the grade at 3 percent or less (2 percent or less, if possible). Calculate the grade by dividing the rise (change in elevation) by the run (length of track): For example, a 3˝ rise in 100˝ of track is 3 percent (3 ÷ 100 = .03, or 3 percent). Steeper grades severely impede operations.

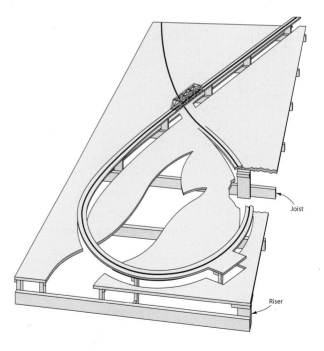

Joist

Riser

Fig. 7-3. Cookie cutter benchwork

chapter eight

Roadbed

Many beginning modelers initially choose to skip roadbed, instead laying track directly on the plywood or other table surface. Unlike real railroads, model railroads don't have to worry about things like drainage,
frost, or heavy trains pushing down through ballast—so why not lay track
directly on a table?

There are many reasons that almost all experienced modelers use roadbed. The main reason is realism: Take a look at a real railroad main line, and notice how the track is higher than the surrounding ground. Model roadbed helps do that. Also note the ballast profile on real railroads, which model railroad roadbed helps simulate.

Also, good trackwork is essential for smooth operation, and model railroad roadbed provides track with a smooth, level surface.

Cork has long been the roadbed of choice for modelers for several reasons: It's easy to cut and bend, it's relatively inexpensive, it's readily available, and it works well.

The first step is to get your track plan transferred to the layout table. It's a good idea to test-fit your track first (especially with sectional track and turnouts) to make sure everything fits according to plan.

If you've never built a layout before, you'll quickly learn that track (especially turnouts) almost always takes up more room on the layout than it did when you were drawing the plan on paper. Make any necessary adjustments before laying roadbed.

Once the track is in place (push pins will hold it in place), you can use it as a guide for marking the track center line, as fig. 8-1 shows.

Cork roadbed comes in 3-foot lengths. Each piece is perforated at an angle down the middle, as shown in fig. 8-2. Pull the pieces apart and turn them so the bevel on each half goes to the outside of the track. You can cut cork with a hobby knife, but a standard utility knife makes cutting it a bit easier.

Fig. 8-1. With the track in place, use a pencil to mark the center line every few ties. Once the track is removed, connect the dots to make a solid center line. This will serve as a guide for laying your roadbed.

Gluing is the best way to secure cork. Do this by running a bead of white glue next to the track center line, as in fig. 8-3. Press the cork in place, and use wire nails or push pins to keep it in place until the glue dries. See fig. 8-4. Once the glue dries, the nails can be removed.

If you decide to nail the cork in place, make sure the heads of the nails are just below the top surface of the cork so that the bottoms of the ties don't rest on them. Any nailheads that stick up can cause uneven track.

Fig. 8-2. Peeling apart the cork will give you two beveled halves.

Fig. 8-3. Run a bead of white glue next to the track center line.

Fig. 8-4. Use wire nails to tack the cork in place until the glue dries. Stagger the joints on each half of the cork.

Fig. 8-5. Cork turnout pads from Midwest and IBL are easy to cut to shape and use.

Lay the other side of the cork like the first. Always stagger joints so that they're not next to each other (fig. 8-4). Also, be sure you don't have a cork joint above a table joint, and likewise avoid track joints directly above cork joints. Doing this will help keep the track as level as possible.

You can do roadbed for turnouts in one of two ways. One is to use precut turnout pads, as fig. 8-5 shows. Available from Midwest and IBL, they can be glued in place with no cutting or fitting required.

However, it's easy to use regular cork strips for turnouts. Doing so only takes a few minutes and will save a few dollars. Start by laying the outside pieces as fig. 8-6 shows. Follow this by adding the inside sections, cutting off the bevel and cutting them to fit. See fig. 8-7. A perfect fit isn't necessary—it's okay to have small gaps at the joints. It's much more important that the top surface be level.

Once the roadbed is in place, sand the top corners of the cork with medium (120-grit) sandpaper, as fig. 8-8 shows. Doing this gets rid of the small lip that often remains along the edge after the roadbed is split apart. If you don't remove this edge, ballast tends to get caught on it, making it difficult to get a smooth ballast profile.

Another popular choice for roadbed is Track-Bed, a black foam rubber product from Woodland Scenics. It is a single-piece, spongy material that is much lighter and softer than cork. See fig. 8-9.

Because it comes as a single piece, you'll need to have an edge line instead of a center line to guide you in laying it. Figure 8-10 shows how to transfer the center line to the edge using a compass.

Since Track-Bed is much spongier than cork, you'll have to be especially careful that you don't drive the track nails down below the surface of the ties. This could cause undulating or uneven track.

Now that you have the roadbed in place, let's move on to the trackwork for your model railroad.

Fig. 8-6. When fabricating a turnout pad, start with the outside pieces.

Fig. 8-7. Cut the two interior pieces to fit.

Fig. 8-8. Use a sanding block with 120-grit sandpaper to remove the burr at the top of the bevel on the cork.

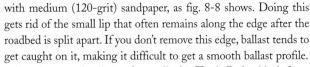

Fig. 8-9. An alternative to cork is Woodland Scenics Track-Bed, a single-piece foam product.

Fig. 8-10. You can draw an edge line for single-piece roadbed using a compass.

chapter nine

Track

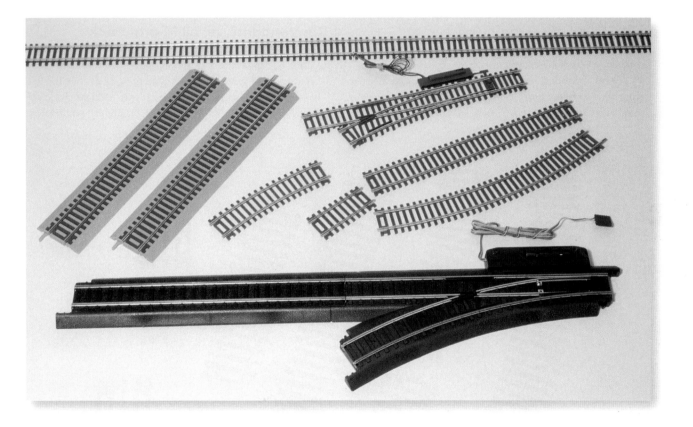

There's a tremendous variety of track on the market today, so much that choosing which type to use can become quite confusing. What will work best for you depends upon how you plan to use it—whether on a permanent layout or a temporary setup—as well as on what you might already have on hand.

Prefabricated model track consists of nickel-silver or brass rail secured to plastic tie strips. Most track these days is made with nickel-silver rail, but you might still come across track with brass rail. If you have the choice, choose nickel-silver. Trains will operate better on nickel-silver than on brass, which tends to oxidize more quickly (impairing electrical contact) and needs cleaning more often.

When you're discussing track, you'll often hear the word "code." It's not a top-secret language. Instead, code refers to the height of the rail in thousandths of an inch. For example, code 100 is .100″ tall; code 83 is .083″; code 70 is .070″; and code 55 is .055″. See fig. 9-1.

Code 100 is common in sectional track. It is the tallest rail made in HO scale, and unfortunately it is quite oversize in scale compared to real rail. Code 83 track has become much more common in recent years, with flextrack, turnouts, and sectional pieces widely available.

Many experienced modelers stick with code 83, which—although it is just a tad heavy in scale compared to most prototype rail—is noticeably more realistic than code 100. It is also easier to cut and work with than code 100, but is still durable. Almost all new equipment will operate on it with no problems.

Code 70 and code 55 are used by some experienced modelers trying to capture the look of branch lines and industrial spurs. Both sizes have a limited supply of components. Micro-

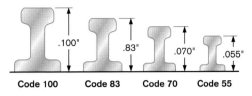

Fig. 9-1. Rail sizes

Engineering makes an excellent line of code 70 turnouts and flextrack, but no sectional components.

If you're just getting started, use code 83 track. It looks good, and there's a wide range of components available. If you've already acquired some code 100 track, don't panic: Walthers makes transition track sections (item no. 948-897) that will allow you to connect code 100 to code 83 track.

Conventional vs. all-in-one track

Let's start with a look at conventional track. Until a few years ago, this was about the only option short of handlaying track.

Track in rigid pieces is known as sectional track. See fig. 9-2. The most common sizes are 9″ lengths of straight track and curves in 18″ radius. Many smaller pieces are also available, as

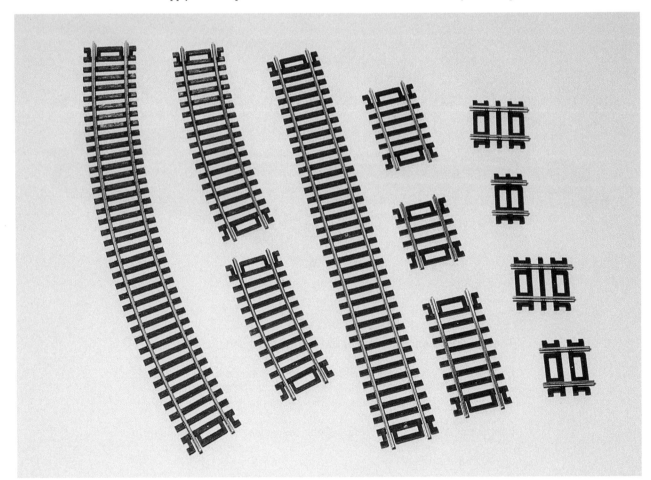

Fig. 9-2. Sectional track comes in a wide variety of lengths in both straight and curved pieces.

Fig. 9-3. Flextrack has gaps in the tie strip beneath the rails, allowing the track to be bent to curves of almost any radius.

Fig. 9-4. The design of all-in-one track varies among manufacturers. The track at left is Atlas True-Track; at right is Life-Like Power-Loc track.

well as curves in 22″, 24″, and other radii, making it possible to build complex track plans.

However, the fixed radius of sectional-track curves can be quite limiting, making it impossible to lay broad curves. As you gain experience and experiment with various track plans, you'll discover the merits of flextrack. See fig. 9-3. Gaps in the plastic tie strips allow flextrack to be curved to almost any radius.

Available in 3-foot (or, in some cases, one-meter) lengths,

flextrack allows long, sweeping curves and also eliminates many track joints, which helps improve operation. A drawback is that it must be cut to fit—a process that isn't difficult, as you'll see later in this chapter.

In recent years track with built-on roadbed has become popular. Many manufacturers offer it, including Atlas True-Track, Bachmann E-Z Track, Kato Unitrack, and Life-Like Power-Loc track. Figure 9-4 shows a couple of samples.

Prototype track

Track in real life consists of heavy steel rail laid on ties. Prototype rail is classified by its weight per yard: 136-pound rail is common in mainline use, 90-pound is typical on branch lines, and even lighter rail is used on spurs and other lightly used areas. Exposure to the elements leaves rail various shades of rust, except for the railhead, which is shiny (provided that it sees regular service).

Treated wood ties are by far the most common, but concrete ties are now used on some heavily used main lines. Ties range from black to various shades of brown and gray, depending upon their age. To keep the rail from biting into the wood, the rail is laid on steel tie plates atop the ties, then spiked in place.

The track structure rests on ballast, which is usually made up of crushed rock of various types and colors. Some branch lines and spurs use cinders instead of rock. The ballast is generally nicely contoured and deep on main lines; on lesser-used lines the ballast isn't as deep and might have weeds and dirt infringing upon it.

The advantage to all-in-one track is that the roadbed is built in (molded in one piece with the ties for some, snapped in place on conventional sectional track for others), so there's no need to lay separate roadbed (such as cork) or ballast the track. It also snaps together (and will hold together) much better without being nailed down than conventional track. It's ideal for temporary layouts or for setting up on tables, carpeted floors, or other irregular surfaces.

One disadvantage is a lack of flexibility—there aren't as many all-in-one track pieces available as there are in standard track. There's no flextrack available, and the design of turnouts makes it difficult to set up conventional passing sidings. Combination roadbed/track is also more expensive than standard track.

Also, unlike conventional sectional and flextrack, all-in-one track from various manufacturers can't be mixed—each maker uses a different style of connectors.

Appearance is also an issue. The all-in-one track pieces don't look as realistic as conventional track that's been ballasted. This can be improved somewhat, as the sidebar on page 54 explains.

So which should you choose? If you've acquired a train set with all-in-one track and want to expand it and try various track arrangements on a table, then buy more all-in-one track of the same brand.

Atlas True-Track is a good choice, because the track sections can be snapped out of the plastic roadbed pieces if you decide to switch to conventional track.

If you're starting with a train set that included conventional track, or if you're planning to build a permanent layout or one with complex trackwork, stick with conventional track. Most experienced modelers, especially those with a couple of layouts under their belts, use conventional track—mainly flextrack with commercial turnouts.

Laying track

It's critical to have a solid connection at every rail joint. Be sure both rails slip into their rail joiners, as in fig. 9-5. If the rails don't match up well, chances are that a rail joiner is bent or loose. Discard it and add a new one.

Figure 9-6 shows the most common mistake in joining track, in which one rail slides over (instead of into) its rail joiner. Check all joints to make sure this doesn't happen.

Make sure joints on curves are tight, as in fig. 9-5. Don't try to force track into a tighter or broader radius, or the result will be an awkward rail angle and a rail gap, as in fig. 9-7. These are a prime source of derailments.

On straight segments of track it's a good idea to leave small gaps every few feet. This allows for expansion and contraction of

Fig. 9-5. Rails should be pushed tightly together, with rail joiners on both rails equally.

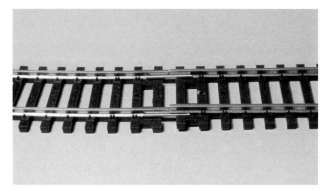

Fig. 9-6. A common mistake is to allow one rail to slide up and over a rail joiner. Pull the track apart and reconnect it properly.

Fig. 9-7. Forcing tracks into a too-tight curve creates a sharp angle and a gapped rail, which will often lead to derailments.

Fig. 9-8. Leave a small rail gap every few feet along straight track to allow for expansion and contraction of the layout.

Fig. 9-9. Use a nail set to drive track nails below rail level.

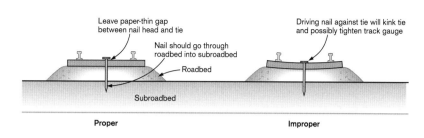

Leave paper-thin gap between nail head and tie

Nail should go through roadbed into subroadbed

Roadbed

Subroadbed

Proper

Driving nail against tie will kink tie and possibly tighten track gauge

Improper

Fig. 9-10. Using track nails.

the layout due to changes in temperature and humidity. Do this only on straight segments (never on curves), as fig. 9-8 shows.

Most sectional track includes holes in ties at each end and in the middle. Use small nails through these holes to secure the track (Atlas track nails work well). See fig. 9-9. Use a small hammer to start the nail, then use a nail set to finish driving the nail below rail-top level. Be sure to keep the nail set vertical—if you hold it at an angle, the nail will bend.

The track nail should go through the roadbed and into the underlying plywood to hold it securely. See fig. 9-10. Also, the head of the nail should just touch the tie. If the nail is driven too far, the tie will be distorted, possibly altering the gauge of the rail.

Some types of track (mainly flextrack and turnouts) include holes in the ties next to the rails for miniature spikes. This is more realistic than track nails. Use needle-nose pliers to push the spikes into place, as in fig. 9-11. Use the side of the jaws to push the spikes against the rails.

Fig. 9-11. Insert spikes into place next to the rail (above left), then use the side of the needle-nose jaws to press the spikes all the way into place (above right). The spikes provide a more realistic look than do track nails (below).

Wire feeders, insulated joiners

You can save yourself some time and headaches later if you know before laying your track where you want track feeders and insulated gaps (read Chapter 10 on wiring for details).

Some train sets include terminal tracks, which have large screw terminals on the side of a piece of sectional track for attaching wires from the power pack. Although they work well, they're unattractive and unrealistic. It's much better to hide electrical connections.

Figure 9-12 shows terminal rail joiners from Atlas. These wire feeders attached to rail joiners eliminate the need to solder feeders directly to the rails. Simply slip the rail joiners into place, drill holes through the roadbed and table for the wires, and slide the track together. You can also solder feeders in place, as shown in Chapter 10.

Insulated rail joiners (fig. 9-13) are used to divide the track into electrical blocks. It's possible to go back later and cut gaps in rails with a razor saw or motor tool (fig. 9-14), but it's easier to use joiners when you lay track.

Laying flextrack

Flextrack is the choice of most experienced modelers building permanent layouts. Flextrack offers several advantages: Each 3-foot length eliminates about three sets of track joints (and their potential problems). It can be bent to nearly any radius, and for curves broader than 24″ flextrack is about the only choice.

Atlas and many other brands of flextrack have holes in ties every

6″ to 8″, much like sectional track. Some flextrack has dimples on the underside of ties that must be drilled out with a small bit. Walthers and Shinohara have holes alongside each rail for spikes every few ties, as fig. 9-11 shows.

Before laying flextrack, you'll have to remove one or two ties from each end to make way for rail joiners. See fig. 9-15.

To lay flextrack, start at one end. For straight sections add one or two track nails or spikes at each end, then go back and add the intermediate spikes or nails as you check the alignment. You can use a long metal straightedge for this, but I find I get the best results by sighting down the rails while installing the intermediate spikes or nails.

Flextrack on curves

The biggest challenge of laying flextrack is that once it's curved, the rail ends don't come out even. This means the inside rail will need to be trimmed to fit. This scares some beginning (and even some intermediate) modelers, but if you follow these steps you'll get a solid rail joint, even on curves.

Start by laying the first piece of flextrack, but don't nail down the last 9″ or so. Bend the end of the track to the proper curve, then mark the long rail at the point that it's even with the shorter one, as fig. 9-16 shows.

Trim the rail with a rail nippers, as fig. 9-17 shows, then use a small fine file to clean any burrs or rough edges. A note on cutting rail: Nothing beats a good rail nipper for doing the job, and Xuron

Fig. 9-12. Terminal rail joiners are easy to use, and they will be nearly invisible when the track is ballasted.

Fig. 9-13. Insulated rail joiners are the easiest way to divide a layout into electrical blocks.

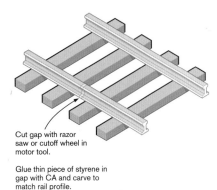

Cut gap with razor saw or cutoff wheel in motor tool.

Glue thin piece of styrene in gap with CA and carve to match rail profile.

Fig. 9-14. Creating rail gaps.

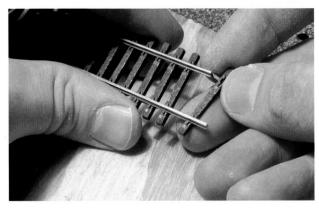

Fig. 9-15. Cut the tie strip under the rail and remove the end tie before laying flextrack.

makes the best I've used. Buy one. The shearing action of the Xuron cutters (the blades slide past each other instead of meeting flush) leaves a clean cut, unlike most standard wire cutters. Razor saws will work, but the process is clumsy and time-consuming (ditto for a cutoff wheel in a motor tool).

Nail or spike the track into place, then slip rail joiners onto the rail ends. Slide the following piece of flextrack into the rail joiners. Once the joint is square, it's time to solder the joints. Apply heat at the joint with a soldering iron (fig. 9-18), keeping the iron in contact with both rails and the rail joiner. Hold the solder to the rail and joiner about ⅛″ from the iron.

As the solder melts into the joint, move the iron back and forth along the joiner, helping the solder melt into the joint. Adding a brushful of flux to the joint before soldering will help the solder penetrate the joint.

Apply the solder to the outside of each rail. That way, any excess solder won't interfere with operations. Fig. 9-19 shows the finished solder joint.

Spike or nail the second piece of flextrack in place, following the same steps as the first. Use a needle file to make sure the tops of the rails make a smooth joint, as fig. 9-20 shows.

To fill in the gap left by the ties that were removed for the rail

Fig. 9-16. Flex the end of the track into position, then mark the long rail at the point where it is even with the other rail end.

Fig. 9-17. Use rail nippers or a razor saw to cut the rail at the mark.

Fig. 9-18. Make sure the joint is tight and square, then solder the rails at each joint.

Fig. 9-19. The finished solder joint should be shiny, with solder along both rails and into the rail joiner.

Fig. 9-20. Give the railhead a couple of passes with a needle file to make sure the joint is smooth.

Fig. 9-21. Finish the joint by filling the gap with a couple of ties under the rail joiners.

Painting track

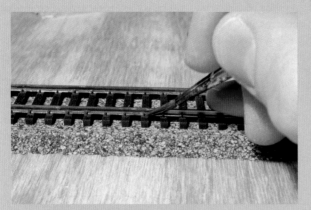 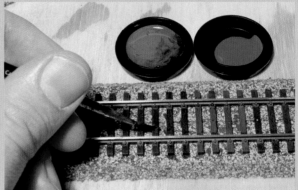

Painting makes model track much more realistic. You can paint track either before or after laying it. Painting it beforehand is often simpler because you can spray it outdoors or in a spray booth, where you don't have to worry about paint fumes.

If you paint it in place, you'll often have some awkward angles to reach. If you do spray the track in place, be sure to open all the windows and provide as much ventilation as possible. Consider wearing a cartridge-style facemask to protect yourself against paint vapors. Spray paints can do serious damage to your lungs and central nervous system.

Start by putting some light oil (such as LaBelle no. 108) on a cloth and wiping the railheads. This will make it much easier to clean the track when you have finished your painting job.

Spray the sides of the rails with a dark rust-colored paint. You can use either a spray can or (if you have access to one) an airbrush. Don't worry much about the name of the paint—just make sure the color is some shade of rust, and that the paint is flat (don't use gloss or satin paints on track). As the photo shows, you can also use a brush—the process will just take longer.

Make sure the sides of the rails are covered, and don't worry if the ties get a coat of paint as well.

The ties are next. Use a brush with various flat colors to paint the ties randomly for realism. I like Polly Scale Engine Black, Grimy Black, Railroad Tie Brown, and Undercoat Light Gray. Once again, don't worry about the name of the paint—just that it dries flat and that the colors look good.

Putting a few drops of each onto a small dish (old film container caps are handy, as the photos show) lets you mix the colors with the brush to get a wide range of colors and effects.

A lightly used branch line or industrial spur should have more light gray, weatherbeaten ties on the track; a heavy-duty main line will have more recently treated, dark-colored ties.

As soon as the paint dries, clean the railheads using a track-cleaning block. If you've oiled the railheads, the dried paint should come off fairly easily.

You can also paint all-in-one track such as this Atlas True-Track, which is handy because the track can be removed and treated like the track above. For the roadbed itself, a wash of black paint (about one part paint to seven or eight parts thinner) will give the roadbed some color variation and make it look more like real ballast. If your track has black roadbed, use a wash of gray paint.

joiners, glue a couple of replacements in place, as fig. 9-21 shows. These can either be low-profile wood ties that have been stained or painted a dark gray to black color, or they can be the cut-away ties with the spike detail carved away to allow them to slip into place.

Turnouts

They're called "switches" on real railroads, and the term is correct for models as well, but over the years they've become known as turnouts to avoid confusion with electrical switches. Figure 9-22 shows the parts of a turnout. Key parts are the points (the movable rails that guide trains to the proper route), the frog (where the two rails meet at a point), throw bar (which connects both points to a throw mechanism), and guard rails (which help wheels follow the proper route).

Turnouts come in different sizes, generally measured by number. The number of a turnout reflects the angle of the diverging track: See fig. 9-22 for a graphic explanation.

Common model turnout sizes are nos. 4, 5, 6, and 8. Number 4 turnouts are considered sharp, with no. 5 intermediate, no. 6 broad, and no. 8 very broad. It's generally wise to use the highest-number turnout possible, because long cars and locomotives will both look and operate much better on broader turnouts.

Some model turnouts aren't numbered. The most common of these is the Atlas Snap-Switch (and similar turnouts from other makers), which is designed to fit in the space of one piece of standard 18″-radius sectional track (and the space of one 9″ piece of straight track). This makes them ideal for use on small layouts, but for larger permanent layouts it's wise to stick to broader-numbered turnouts.

Curved turnouts are also available. Figure 9-23 shows one from Walthers. These are designated by the radius of the inner and outer tracks.

Model turnouts are available either with insulated frogs or with metal uninsulated frogs, and each requires different wiring considerations. Chapter 10 explains the differences and lists the manufacturers of each.

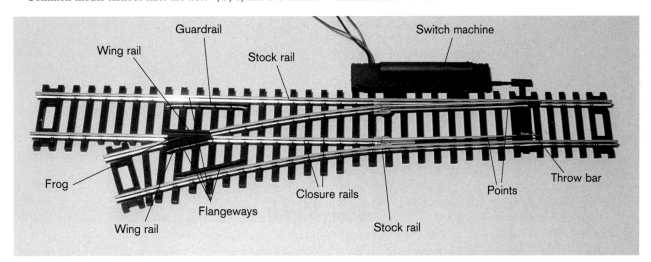

Fig. 9-22. Turnout parts

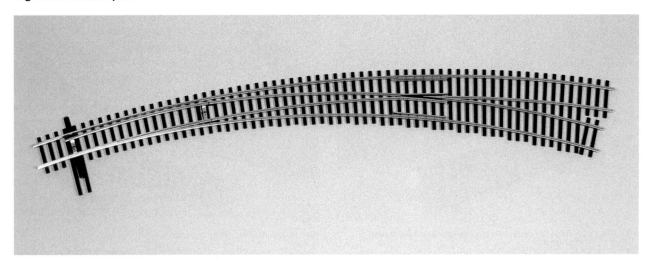

Fig. 9-23. This Walthers code 83 no. 8 is an example of a curved turnout.

Controlling turnouts

Turnouts are thrown either manually or by remote control. Manual turnouts are controlled by hand at the turnout itself, while remote control turnouts are powered by a switch machine and can be controlled by an electrical switch on a control panel or the layout fascia.

Manual turnouts from Atlas, Life-Like, and others often include a manual switch machine (controlled with a slide switch) on the turnout. They look like the machine in fig. 9-22, without the wires. Although they work fine, their appearance leaves a lot to be desired. They are bulky and don't look like anything found on a real switch. Fortunately, on most turnouts they are not necessary and can be easily removed.

One of the simplest (and least expensive) alternatives to the bulky manual switch is a handmade spring, as shown in fig. 9-24. It can be made from a short piece of piano wire or a paper clip. Drill holes in the throw bar and in a neighboring tie as shown, and insert the spring.

Fig. 9-24. This simple spring will hold a turnout in either direction. Make sure that the end of the spring that goes into the tie extends well into the roadbed.

Fig. 9-25. The throw mechanism on this Caboose Industries ground throw connects to the turnout throw bar.

Fig. 9-26. Slow-motion machines like this under-table Tortoise use a motor to throw the control wire back and forth.

Fig. 9-27. These Atlas twin-coil machines are both designed for under-table mounting.

Fig. 9-28. If you plan to use under-table switch machines, drill a ½" hole through the table and roadbed under the center of the turnout throw bar before laying track.

The turnout can now be thrown simply by sliding the points back and forth. The spring provides positive action, holding the points securely in the direction thrown.

Another alternative is to use a manual ground throw. Caboose Industries and N. J. International make a wide line of ground throws. They are large compared to prototype switch stands, but are more realistic than the factory-installed controls. See fig. 9-25.

Remote control switch machines are handy in many situations, especially where a turnout is difficult to reach. Many modelers use switch machines on all turnouts, to avoid the possible damage that can occur when operators reach into the layout to throw a turnout.

There are two basic types of switch machines: twin-coil and motor. Twin-coil switch machines have two solenoids (one for each direction). Power to them is normally off—they require just a momentary zap of electricity to move the throw rod into place. Continuous current will damage them. Makers of twin-coil machines include Atlas, Life-Like, Roco, and others.

Motor-type switch machines—also known as slow-motion machines—are controlled by changing the polarity in a low-current-draw motor. The motor slowly moves the throw rod, then stalls at the limit of its motion. This doesn't damage this type of motor, so power is on at all times. Slow-motion machines include the Tortoise, Peco, SwitchMaster, and others.

Switch machines can be mounted either above the table or below the table. Above-table switch machines, such as the Atlas in fig. 9-22, simply don't look realistic. Under-table machines, such as the Tortoise in fig. 9-26 or the Atlas machines in fig. 9-27, are the best choice.

It's best if you can decide what type of machine you'll be using prior to laying your track. Most under-table machines use a rod routed through the layout table and roadbed into the turnout's throw bar. This requires a hole to be drilled under the throw bar as in fig. 9-28.

Chapter 10 provides details on switch machine wiring.

Keeping track clean

Clean track is vital to smooth operation. When track gets dirty it impairs electrical contact, which can result in jerky operation. Dirty track will also lead to dirty wheels, which lead to yet more electrical contact problems.

The best way to keep track clean is also the most fun: Run lots of trains! The more frequently you run trains, the cleaner the rails will stay.

Clean track is also a function of where a layout is located. Areas such as unfinished basements, attics, and garages, or rooms with open windows will have a great deal of dust, which will find its way to the track. Layouts in finished, enclosed areas will have comparatively fewer dust and grime problems. Also be aware that smoking near a layout results in residue on the track that inhibits electrical contact and can be difficult to clean.

The most common track cleaners are track-cleaning blocks such as the Walthers Bright Boy and Roco 10002 cleaner, shown in fig. 9-29. To use them, rub them along the railheads. Be careful around switch points, which can easily be damaged. See fig. 9-30.

Several companies also make track-cleaning cars. The two you're most likely to find in hobby shops are the Aztec and Centerline, both shown in fig. 9-29. The Aztec car uses a cylindrical abrasive rubber roller—similar to the material in a Bright Boy—to scrub the rails.

The Centerline car has a cloth wrapped around a heavy brass roller. The cloth is soaked in a track-cleaning liquid (such as Goo-Gone) and pulled around the layout. Some modelers use a second car with a dry cloth following the first to help pick up any residual gunk.

Now that your track is in good running shape, let's take a look at wiring your layout.

Fig. 9-29. Clockwise from lower left: Centerline track-cleaning car, Life-Like liquid track cleaner, Aztec track-cleaning car, Roco track cleaning block, Walthers Bright Boy cleaning block.

Fig. 9-30. Rub the track-cleaning block on the railheads, taking care around turnouts and other delicate trackwork.

From track plan to benchwork

You've managed to find the perfect track plan in a book or magazine, or you've spent hours at the drawing table or computer carefully drafting a track plan. The next step is transferring the track plan to your layout table or benchwork.

If you've never done this before, the first thing you'll probably learn is that—regardless of how carefully you've measured—track will almost always take up more room on the layout than it did on paper.

Tools and tricks

One of the first steps in track planning is drawing a grid on the layout top. As fig. 1 shows, a drywall T-square with a four-foot arm is invaluable for this. A 12" grid is usually sufficient, but for complex plans you might want to add grid lines at the 6" marks as well. It's also important to draw grid lines on the track plan to match those on your layout surface.

Once the grid is drawn on the layout and track plan, the next step is to mark out the radii of curves. Figure 2 shows how to find and mark the center of the radii on the track plan. Transfer the center point to the layout table, then use a compass to transfer the curve to the table.

You can make a compass by using an old wood yardstick. Holes in the yardstick at 1" intervals make handy guides for a pencil. However, some curves are too broad to easily use a yardstick, or the center of the curve may be well off the layout table. In this case curve templates work well (see fig. 3).

My curve templates are about 40" long and made from large pieces of .060" styrene that I had on hand. You can also make them from hardboard (such as Masonite) or thin plywood. Cardboard will work, but it is not as durable as hardboard. I made my templates in 2" intervals from 18" to 44", and as the photo shows, there is a different radius on each side of the template.

Planning turnouts

Probably the most difficult part of track planning is leaving enough room for turnouts. They always seem to take up more space than originally figured, and every manufacturer's turnouts vary slightly in size and shape. Because of this, complex trackwork in published plans often doesn't fit the same way on a layout.

To remove the guesswork, make several paper turnout templates by placing turnouts on a photocopier, then running off as many copies as you need. Be sure to label them with the brand name and size.

As you use templates, tape them in place, as shown in fig. 4. Alignment is the important thing—remember that you can trim turnouts to fit tighter areas as long as you maintain proper alignment and track center spacing.

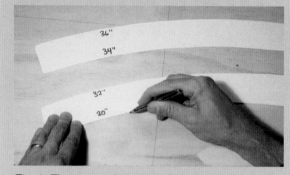

Fig. 1. A drywall T-square with a four-foot arm works well for laying out a grid on the table.

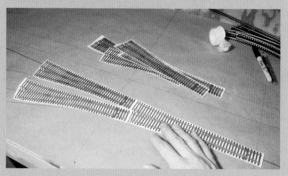

Fig. 2. Measure to find the center point of each curve, then mark it on the track plan.

Fig. 3. These templates, made from styrene, hardboard, or thin plywood, are handy for drawing broad curves.

Fig. 4. While trimming turnouts to size, tape templates in place to prevent the track from becoming misaligned.

Wiring

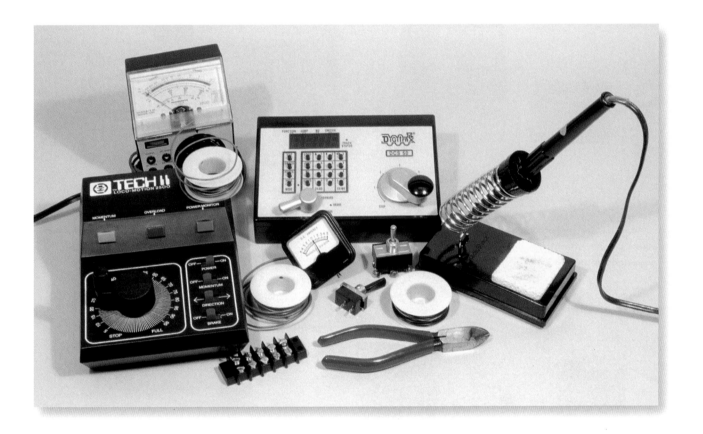

Electricity intimidates many modelers, but having a basic knowledge of electricity and how it works will take away some of the fear of wiring a layout. Most wiring challenges in model railroading aren't difficult to figure out—it's usually a matter of breaking things down into smaller steps. Let's start with a basic overview of electricity.

Basics

Electricity is either alternating current (AC) or direct current (DC). With alternating current the electrons are continually changing directions. With direct current the electrons flow in one direction, creating positive (+) and negative (-) properties.

Electricity is measured in volts (V) and amperes (A), or amps. Volts are a measure of the force of electricity, while amps measure the amount of energy being used. House current in the U.S. is 120V AC, but scale trains in HO scale operate on DC, and at a much lower voltage—about 12 volts at top speed.

To run trains you'll need a power pack, which reduces the voltage and converts the electricity to DC. See fig. 10-1. Most train sets include small power packs, and good-quality power packs are available separately from Model Rectifier Corp. (MRC), Bachmann, and others.

Figure 10-2 shows the outputs found on a typical power pack.

The variable DC terminals connect to the track, which is controlled by the control knob. Almost all packs have a fixed AC terminal for accessories; some, like this MRC pack, have fixed DC terminals as well.

Running one train is as simple as connecting the wires from the power pack to the tracks. Turn the knob on the controller, and the train will begin to move. Stop the train, flip the reversing (direction) switch, turn up the dial again, and the train will go in the opposite direction.

No special wiring is needed to operate two or more locomotives on a single train. Track polarity determines which way a locomotive will go, regardless of which way the engine actually points.

When running multiple engines, make sure your power pack can handle the increased current draw. Power packs are usually rated in volt-amps (VA), which can be determined by multiplying volts by amps. For example, a pack rated at 12 volt-amps can

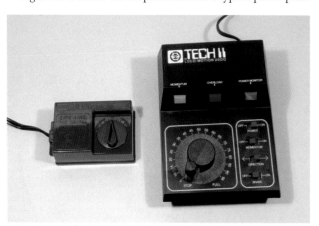

Fig. 10-1. Power packs reduce house current to low-voltage DC for trains. The pack at left is from a Life-Like train set; the MRC pack at right has many advanced features.

Fig. 10-2. All packs have a variable DC output for trains; most have an AC output for accessories, and some have an additional fixed DC output for accessories.

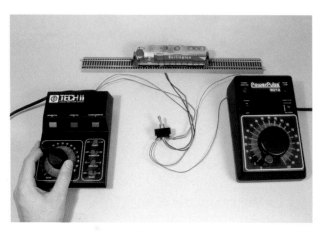

Fig. 10-3. Cab control—the basics.

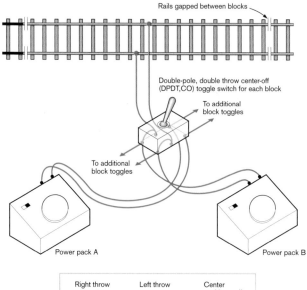

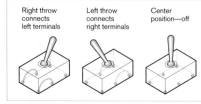

deliver 1 ampere at 12 volts. The average HO locomotive draws just under .5A (although many newer models draw much less, and some older models draw more), so such a power pack could handle two (possibly three) locomotives. Overloading a pack will result in slow operation and could cause the pack to overheat.

If you have a small train-set power pack, consider upgrading to a new one. One advantage to a new pack is power. For example, the train-set pack in fig. 10-1 is rated at just 7VA, while the MRC Tech II pack is rated at 16VA. Other advantages of a quality power pack are smoother speed control with a 270-degree (or greater) control knob, pilot lamp, automatic overload protection, and a separate power on/off switch.

Some advanced packs also have momentum features that simulate the drag of a train by gradually increasing and decreasing the speed to follow adjustments on the control knob, as well as a button to simulate train braking.

If you buy a new pack, don't throw the old one away—it will work well for powering switch machines, lamps, and other accessories.

Running two trains at once

On medium-size and larger layouts it can be fun to run two or more trains at once with separate power packs. The most common way to do this is known as cab control. With cab control, the layout is electrically divided into sections called blocks. Each block is controlled by a double-pole, double-throw (DPDT) center-off toggle switch. Operators can throw the toggle left or right to select either power pack. Figure 10-3 shows the basic idea.

You'll need a toggle switch for each block, and you'll need to provide gaps in the rails between blocks. The easiest way of doing this is with insulated rail joiners, as was explained in the chapter on trackwork (chapter 9).

Run the two wires from the first power pack to the two terminals on the opposite side of each toggle switch, as fig. 10-4 shows. Do the same with the second power pack. Then connect the two center terminals from each block toggle to the track for that block.

Cab control's advantage is that it's relatively simple to do, regardless of the layout size: Adding more blocks is just a matter of adding more toggle switches and connecting them to your power packs.

A disadvantage is that cab control can use a lot of wire, especially on a larger layout. Also, while running trains you and the other operator must be very conscious of where your train is in relation to the block boundaries.

Even if you decide to stick to a single power pack, you'll find it handy to be able to store locomotives (or trains) in spurs and sidings while you're running another train. To do this, create a block by gapping a rail and control it with a single on/off (single-pole, single-throw) toggle switch, as fig. 10-5 shows.

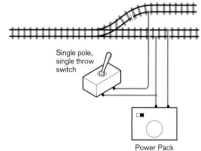

Fig. 10-5. On-off control for spur.

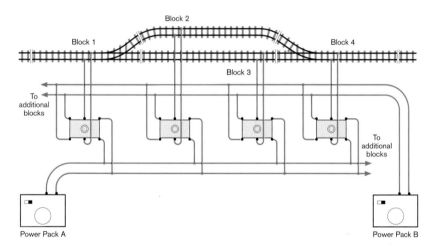

Fig. 10-4. Cab control—multiple blocks.

Digital Command Control

Command control—in which multiple operators can control their trains anywhere on a layout without regard to electrical blocks—has been around since the 1960s. However, in the past few years the components have become small enough, inexpensive enough, and easy enough to use to make command control a popular choice among even beginning modelers.

Digital Command Control (DCC) is a form of command control that follows NMRA guidelines, with standards allowing companies to make components compatible with other systems.

DCC is the ultimate in train control. Figure 10-6 provides an overview. The key to DCC is that track power is always on, and each locomotive has a small circuit board, called a decoder, that picks up signals from the track. Each decoder has its own unique address, so it selects from the track only the signals intended for it. Hand-held throttles (several can be used at once) communicate with the command station, which in turn sends signals to the track.

In theory, DCC requires just two wires to the track, doing away with all the toggle switches and additional block wiring required of cab control. In reality it's a bit more complex than that, but there's still much less wiring required than with block control.

The best way to distribute power is by using a track bus of at least 16-gauge wire. Install track feeders to every individual section of rail if possible (or at least every 36″) to keep the DCC signal strong. A weak signal can cause poor, erratic operation.

Depending upon the size of the layout, multiple power stations can be used to distribute electricity. Dividing a layout into two or more sections this way also makes troubleshooting easier when problems develop.

Figure 10-7 shows a basic Digitrax DCC system. High-quality DCC systems are also made by Atlas, CVP Products, Lenz, North Coast, MRC, and Wangrow.

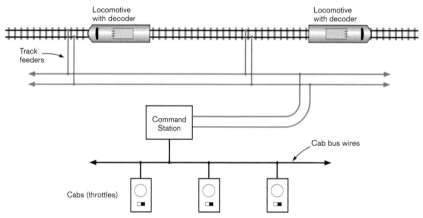

Fig. 10-6. Digital command control overview.

Fig. 10-7. The Digitrax Zephyr is a basic DCC system. Several hand-held throttles can be used at once to run multiple trains.

Fig. 10-8. This Atlas SD35 has a DCC decoder built into its circuit board. Moving the plug at right allows modelers to switch from DCC to standard DC control.

Decoders

Some manufacturers now offer the option of factory-installed DCC decoders in their locomotives, such as the Atlas SD35 in fig. 10-8. Most other new models are sold as "DCC-ready," a somewhat vague term that can mean anything from having a socket for a plug-in decoder to having a circuit board that can easily be replaced by a circuit-board-style decoder.

Key decoder properties include their amperage ratings and the number of function outputs. New HO locomotives typically draw well under .5A; some older locomotives draw above .5A. In general, .5A to 1A decoders are sufficient for HO scale locomotives.

Function outputs are used to control headlights (separate front and rear on most diesels), ditch lights, and warning lights.

Basic decoder installation

The easiest installations are those on locomotives that are labeled "DCC-ready." A socket-style locomotive is shown in fig. 10-9. The Proto 2000 diesel has a DIP (dual in-line) socket; others have straight in-line sockets. Check the instructions that come with each locomotive for specific details—some models require installation of lower-voltage headlights in place of the factory-installed bulbs when adding DCC.

Some locomotives have a dummy plug in the socket that must be removed and replaced with a decoder; on others, like the one in fig. 10-9, the circuit board itself is removed and the decoder then plugged in place. The arrow on the circuit board indicates where the connection for the orange wire on the plug should go. If you get it backward at first, don't worry—reverse the connection and try again.

Another fairly easy conversion is with circuit-board-style decoders, as on the Stewart F unit in fig. 10-10. They require removal of the factory-installed circuit board. The new circuit board then drops into place. Doing this requires disconnecting and reconnecting wires from the wheel pickups and headlights.

Older locomotives (and some new ones) aren't DCC ready. Decoders must be hard-wired into them, a process that goes beyond the scope of this book.

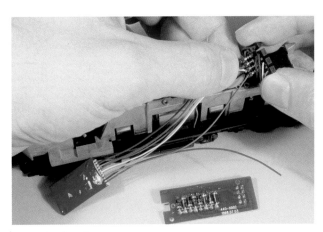

Fig. 10-9. Adding a DCC decoder to this Proto 2000 GP9 was a simple matter of removing the original plug and circuit board, then plugging the decoder into place.

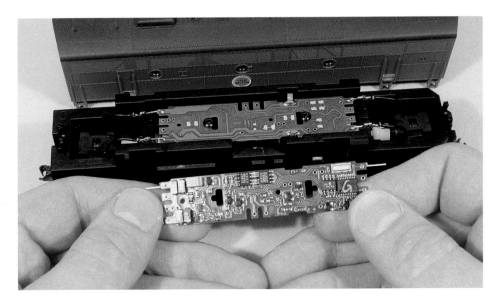

Fig. 10-10. Adding a decoder to this Stewart Hobbies F unit involved removing the original circuit board and screwing this new circuit-board-style decoder in place. The engine connection tabs and track wires had to be removed and then reinstalled.

Reverse loops

You must be conscious of reverse loops whenever you're designing a layout or setting up track, regardless of whether you're using a single power pack, cab control, or DCC. Reverse loops require special wiring and gapping rails to avoid short circuits, as fig. 10-11 shows.

The simple return loop is the most obvious (and most common) type of reverse loop, but there are other types as well: fig. 10-12 shows other variations.

Wiring for reverse loops isn't difficult, but it does take a bit of planning. The basic idea is to isolate the loop itself and use a switch or switches to change the polarity while a train is in the loop.

Figure 10-13 shows two methods of wiring a return loop—one uses a single double-pole, double-throw (DPDT) toggle switch; the second method uses two switches. The one-switch method is a bit easier to wire, but trickier to operate. The two-switch method takes a bit more time to wire but is simple to operate.

With the one-switch method you must set the loop direction switch to match the polarity of the main line. The train can then enter the loop. When the train is in the loop, you throw the power pack's reversing switch to allow the train to continue out of the loop, back onto the main line.

This gets tricky, because the loop direction switch isn't independent of the power pack switch, so polarity of the pack must be changed while the train is in the loop. This means you either have to stop the train while throwing both switches, or you have to throw both switches at the same time (and if you miss on the timing the train will jerk).

The one-switch method works well with Digital Command Control, because the locomotive's direction is based on a command signal rather than track polarity.

The two-switch method is usually best for standard DC layouts. As shown in fig. 10-13, the additional switch is the main direction switch. This lets you change the polarity of the main line independently of the reversing section, eliminating the need for stopping (or throwing two switches at once) while the train is in the loop.

A potential problem is that it's impossible for an operator to tell which route the polarity is aligned for. A simple solution is to use a pair of green 16V bulbs, as fig. 10-14 shows. Place them on the control panel next to their corresponding routes. Whichever is lighted indicates the correct route.

There are other ways to control loops, some automatically, but they go beyond the scope of this book. For a more in-depth look at wiring, see *Easy Model Railroad Wiring, Second Edition*, by Andy Sperandeo (Kalmbach Publishing Co.).

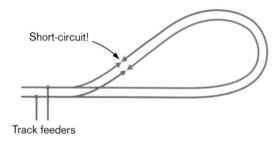

Fig. 10-11. Reverse loop.

Turnout brand	Standard	Power-routing
Atlas	X	
Bachmann	X	
Kato	Optional	Optional
Life-Like	X	
Micro Engineering		X
Peco ElectroFrog		X
Peco InsulFrog	X	
Roco		X
Shinohara		X
Walthers		X

Return loop

Wye

Cutoff track

Fig. 10-12. Types of reverse loops.

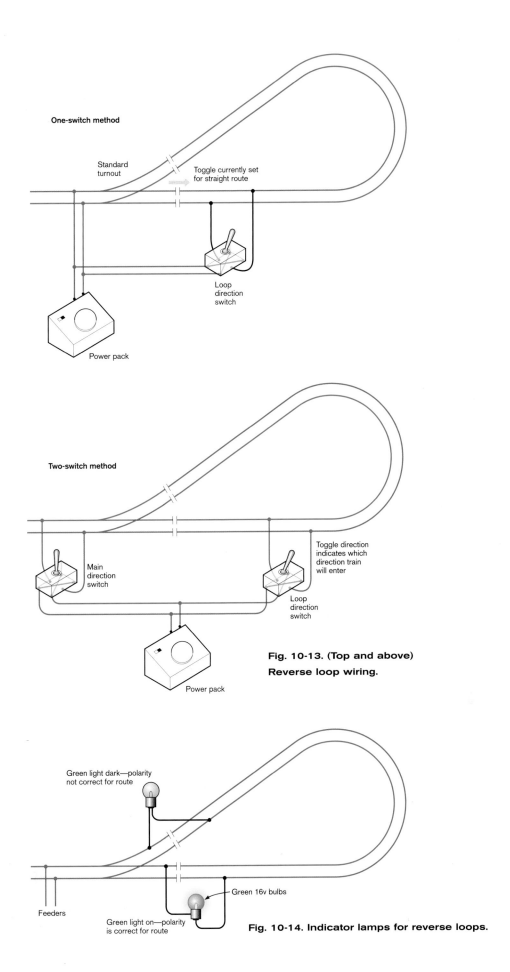

One-switch method

Standard turnout

Toggle currently set for straight route

Loop direction switch

Power pack

Two-switch method

Main direction switch

Toggle direction indicates which direction train will enter

Loop direction switch

Power pack

Fig. 10-13. (Top and above) Reverse loop wiring.

Green light dark—polarity not correct for route

Green 16v bulbs

Feeders

Green light on—polarity is correct for route

Fig. 10-14. Indicator lamps for reverse loops.

Turnouts: standard and power-routing

Turnouts come in two basic types: standard and power-routing (sometimes called selective). Figure 10-15 illustrates the differences and lists the makers of each type of turnout.

On standard turnouts the frog is electrically isolated (dead) and both routes are live at all times. No special wiring is necessary for standard turnouts.

With power-routing turnouts the frog is always live. Throwing the turnout changes the polarity of the frog to match the route selected. The route not selected is electrically dead.

When using power-routing turnouts, you must follow two rules to avoid short circuits. First, place gaps in the rails between turnouts located frog-to-frog. Second, locate track feeders off the point ends of turnouts—never off the frog end. Figure 10-16 illustrates both principles.

Switch machine control

If you use electric switch machines as described in Chapter 9, you'll need to control them. It's best if you can provide a separate power supply for turnouts (such as an old power pack or plug-in wall transformer). Using the accessory terminals on a power pack that's also being used to run trains can take power away from the trains. Also, throwing a twin-coil machine while a train is running can make the train suddenly hesitate.

Figure 10-17 shows two ways of wiring twin-coil machines (the kind that snap a turnout's points into place). Examples include those made by Atlas, Life-Like, and Roco. Twin-coil machines need a momentary shot of electricity to work. If power is fed continually to them, they'll overheat and burn out.

The Atlas switch controllers (and clones) that come with many of these switch machines will work fine; a disadvantage is that they can't be located on a track schematic on a control panel.

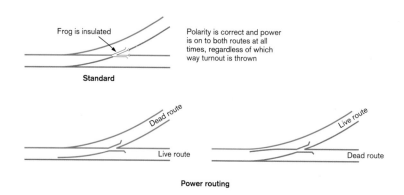

Fig. 10-15. Types of turnouts.

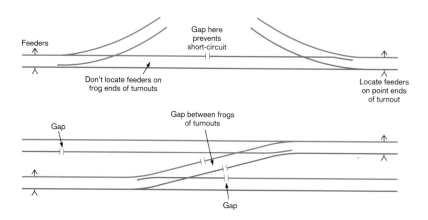

Fig. 10-16. Wiring with power-routing turnouts.

Control panels

Control panels are handy for centralizing toggle switches for block control, as well as switches for controlling turnouts and accessories. For small layouts a central control panel, with all controls on it, works well. For larger layouts smaller local control panels can be located around the layout near the sections they control.

The photos show one way of making a control panel using ⅛" hardboard. Cut the hardboard to shape, then paint the board white. Use narrow masking tape to create a schematic of the track. Press the tape firmly into place, then spray the panel with black or another contrasting color. Peeling up the masking tape leaves the track pattern in white on the panel.

Drill holes at appropriate locations for mounting switches and lamps as needed. The panel can be mounted vertically to the edge of the layout, or table-style. Lettering can be added with dry-transfer or decal alphabet sets.

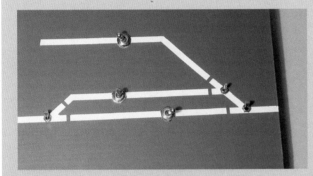

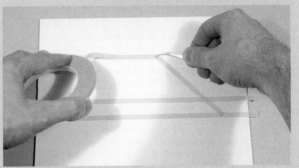

The other option is to use momentary-contact push buttons, as the top portion of fig. 10-17 shows. The wiring for this is simple, and the push buttons can be located directly on the turnout schematic on a control panel.

Slow-motion (stall-motor) machines use a motor to drive the actuating lever. The low-current-draw motor is designed to stall as it reaches the limit of the throw and can have power going to it at all times. Examples are the Circuitron Tortoise, Switchmaster, and Peco.

Figure 10-18 shows the simplest way of wiring slow-motion stall-motor machines using a DC power supply. Using small double-pole, double-throw toggle switches is handy, because they also serve to indicate the direction the turnout is thrown. See the sidebar on control panels on page 67

Accessories

Wiring accessories, such as structure lights and streetlights, is fairly straightforward. Figure 10-19 shows an example. Make sure that the lamps and other accessories are rated higher than your power supply—in other words, if your streetlights have 16V bulbs, make sure the power supply is less than 16V.

Running lamps a couple of volts less than their rated voltage is a good idea. They will shine almost as brightly, and bulb life will be significantly increased.

It's a good idea to use a separate power supply for your accessories, like switch machines, to avoid taking power away from running trains.

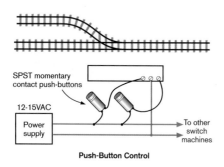

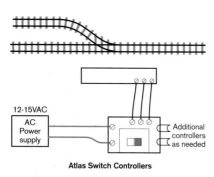

Fig. 10-17. Controlling twin-coil switch machines

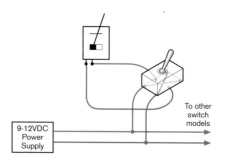

Fig. 10-18. Controlling small-motor switch machines

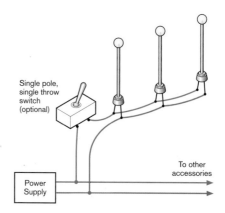

Fig. 10-19. Accessory wiring.

Mechanics of wiring

Wire comes in several sizes and is of two main types: solid and stranded. See fig. 10-20. Wire is measured by gauge: the smaller the number, the larger the wire. For comparison, household wire is 12 or 14 gauge; track feeders can be 22 or 24 gauge, and 16 gauge is a good size for main bus (power supply) wires and switch machine power.

Stranded wire is designed for applications in which the wire is subject to repeated movement or bending. For all other applications, choose solid wire.

Regardless of which control method you use, you'll need to master a few skills and tools to join wires together. Soldering is usually the best method of joining wires together, because it provides a solid mechanical connection.

A small (25- or 30-watt) pencil-type iron, as shown in fig. 10-21, works well for most applications. Keep the tip filed to a chisel point. If the tip becomes dirty or pitted, use a flat mill file to reshape the tip. After filing the tip (or if the tip is new), you must tin it. Do this by letting the iron get hot, then touching solder to it.

Keep a damp (not wet) sponge handy (the stand in fig. 10-21 has a place for one), and wipe the tip often on it to keep the tip clean during use.

Fig. 10-20. Common wire includes, from left, 14-gauge solid, 22-gauge solid, and two-conductor 24-gauge speaker wire.

Fig. 10-21. A 25-watt pencil-type soldering iron works well for most model railroad applications.

Multimeter

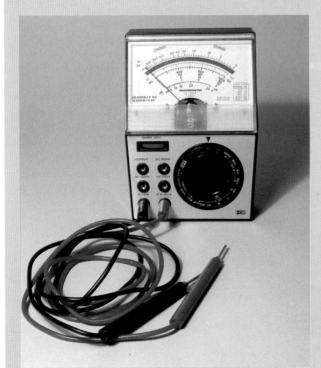

A multimeter is a handy tool to have when wiring. Multimeters can check AC or DC volts, current draw, and resistance. If a locomotive is not running or is behaving erratically, you can use a multimeter to make sure that power is reaching the track. You can also use it to check voltage and current draw of various accessories.

When you're checking voltage, do so in parallel (across the wires in a circuit). When you're checking amps, you need to do it in series.

The ohmmeter (resistance) function is handy for tracing short circuits—it will tell you if a circuit is open or closed. This is handy with both trackwork and wiring.

Don't wire a multimeter permanently in a circuit. Continuous current will damage the milliammeter portion of the meter's circuitry.

Always use resin-core solder for wiring. Don't use acid-core solder, as electricity flowing through an acid-core solder joint will cause it to corrode. Solder with a 60/40 tin/lead content is ideal for wiring, although there are now several types of lead-free solder on the market.

Start by joining the wires to be soldered. Figure 10-22 shows an end-to-end joint; fig. 10-23 shows a T-joint.

Strip the wires in the areas to be soldered. Slip shrink-wrap insulation over one of the wires if desired (fig. 10-24), then wrap the wires securely to each other.

Press the tip of the hot iron to the joint, being sure to contact both wires. See fig. 10-22. Touch the solder to the wires (not to the iron), and the solder will flow into the joint. When the solder flows through the entire joint, remove the iron and let the joint cool. The solder should have a bright, shiny appearance.

Don't move the joint while the solder is still liquid, or the joint will be weak and have a crystallized appearance. If this happens, reheat the joint until the solder melts, then let the joint cool.

Insulate all solder joints with shrink-wrap insulation or electrical tape. Fig. 10-24 shows how to use the side of a soldering iron tip to shrink the insulation in place over a joint.

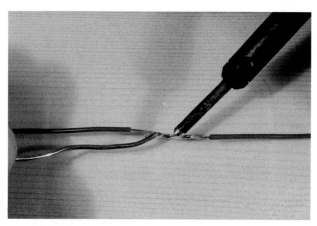

Fig. 10-22. Heat both wires with the iron while holding the solder to the wires away from the iron. When the solder begins to melt, it will flow through the entire joint.

Fig. 10-23. Here's a T-joint. A good joint will be shiny, with solder surrounding all wires in the joint.

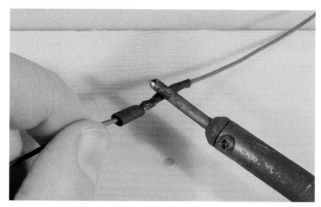

Fig. 10-24. Slip shrink-wrap insulation onto the wire before joining the wires. Slide the insulation over the joint, then rub it with the side of a soldering iron tip to shrink the insulation firmly onto the joint.

Basics of wire

Knowing what different types of wire can do, what tools and connectors are available, and what connection options you have can help you wire your layout.

Work toward two goals when wiring: First, ensure that circuits never have a reason to fail. Second, organize circuits to make later modifications or repairs easier.

Wire

Insulated copper wire (fig. 1) is the standard for electrical wiring. Wire has two descriptors: size and type (stranded or solid). The size is measured in gauge and indicated by a number, as in 22AWG (American Wire Gauge). The smaller the number, the larger (in diameter) the wire, and the more current it can handle. Most 120V (volt) household wiring is 12- and 14-gauge. Either will work well for track and other main power supply wires. Smaller wire, such as 20 gauge, is okay for track feeders, but shouldn't be used for long runs.

Solid wire is preferred for most applications. It's easy to prepare for soldering and can be used with crimp-on terminals. Use stranded wire where flexibility is important.

Wire cutters and strippers

Several tools are necessary for working with wire. A good pair of cutters (see fig. 2) will stay sharp for a long time, but never use them to cut steel wire or the cutting edge will be damaged. A wire stripper is indispensible.

They make an otherwise tedious job fast and easy. Crimping tools enable you to use many types of wire connectors. Many strippers are combined with a crimping tool, such as the one in fig. 2.

Spade and other connectors

Whenever a wire needs to be connected to a screw terminal you can add a spade connector as in fig. 3. Strip the end of the wire, ensuring none of the bare wire is exposed beyond the connector. Slip the spade into place, then use a crimping tool to fasten it. Terminal strips are available in many shapes and sizes. They're great for simplifying wiring on modular or sectional layouts and can minimize solder joints on other layouts. Suitcase or tap-in connectors (fig. 4) allow you to connect a feeder into a bus wire without having to strip either wire.

Keep it neat

It's tempting to make wire runs as short as possible, but this can create a rat's nest under a layout. I like to route the main track power wires under the main line to keep the track feeders as short as possible.

Label all of your wires, and color-code everything. When routing wires, use wire staples to hold the wires in place. Using ordinary staples or wire nails crimped over wires can cut into and damage wire, leading to short circuits and other failures.

Fig. 1. A sampling of available wire: 14-gauge solid, 18-gauge stranded, 22-gauge solid, and two-conductor 24-gauge solid (speaker wire).

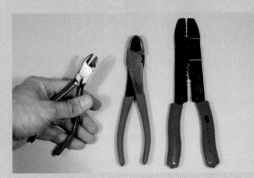

Fig. 2. Small (6") and large (8") wire cutters and a stripper/crimper are vital for working with wire.

Fig. 3. Add spade terminals by threading them onto the stripped end and crimping them in place.

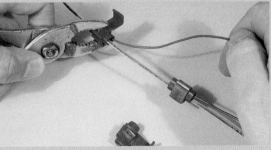

Fig. 4. Suitcase connectors: use a channel lock to push the metal strip in place, then close the cover.

chapter eleven

Structures

This Bachmann drugstore has been dressed up with a paint job as well as signs and interior details.

A tremendous variety of structure kits may be found on the market. These range from small storefront structures to huge industrial buildings—and even full complexes.

Unlike freight cars and locomotives, the majority of structures come in kit form. The good news is that most structure kits you'll find in a hobby shop are relatively easy to assemble, making them a great place to start gaining experience in model building.

Most kits are made of either injection-molded styrene or wood parts. Plastic kits have long been regarded as the easiest to put together, but in the past decade wood kits with laser-cut pieces have become popular, with pieces cut to size and tab-and-slot construction.

There are also plenty of craftsman kits on the market. Traditional craftsman kits are generally made up of wood, resin, or plaster components, and assembling them requires lots of cutting and fitting. I'd suggest starting with a few basic plastic or wood kits before moving on to complex structures.

Basic kit construction

Let's follow the assembly process of a basic plastic kit—in this case Crown Paint & Hardware from Walthers. Figure 11-1 shows what you get when you open the box. It's a basic storefront building, but it includes separate window frame castings and a multipart front.

Before starting construction, determine how you want the finished kit to appear. Most structures benefit greatly from a coat of paint—a necessity for wood kits. Painting might not appear necessary for plastic kits, because many of them are molded in several colors. My advice is to paint all surfaces, and ignore the kit box if it states "no painting necessary." Painting will kill the plastic shine found on many kits and will result in a much more realistic structure.

Many structures (including this one) include a base, but I often don't use it. You'll find it's often easier to blend a structure into the scenery if it doesn't have a base. In this case I wanted the

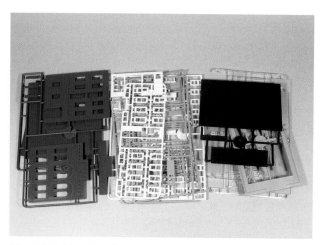

Fig. 11-1. Here's what you can expect to see after opening a typical plastic structure kit.

storefront building to sit directly on the sidewalk, so a base below the structure would simply get in the way.

It's wise to assemble a structure kit as much as you can before painting. With plastic kits especially, this reduces the chance that plastic cement will ooze out of joints and wreck the paint.

Start by cutting the main wall sections from their sprues. Structures have different ways of meeting at the corners: Some have butt-joint walls, some have separate corner pieces, and some—like this one—have 45-degree bevels at each corner. Whatever the construction method, test-fit the joints to make sure they fit snugly. See fig. 11-2. If not, use a hobby knife to trim any flash or stray material out of the way until the walls fit properly.

Glue two of the wall sections together, as fig. 11-3 shows. Run a bead of plastic cement along one of the mating pieces, then press the other piece in place. Hold the pieces together (standing them

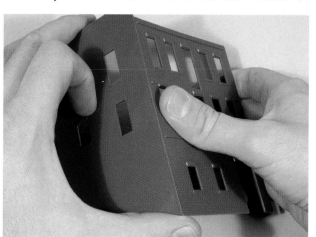

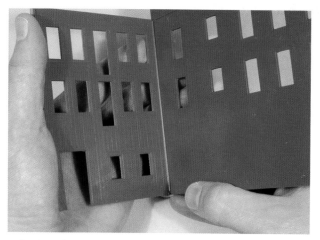

Fig. 11-2. Test-fit the corners to make sure they fit snugly against each other. This structure includes an extra lip on the rear of one wall to help locate the neighboring wall.

on the workbench works well) until the glue begins to set. Follow this by adding a brushful of liquid plastic cement into the joint from behind. Make sure the pieces stay aligned, then leave them alone to dry.

In the meantime, do the other pair of walls. When the joints in both subassemblies have set securely, join the two sections one joint at a time.

Some structures don't include much in the way of support at the corners. If this is the case, add a reinforcing strip of square styrene, as fig. 11-4 shows. Adding this strip to one wall before joining the two walls will make it easier to add the second wall.

On the Walthers structure the lower front portion of the front wall is made up of four separate sections. It represents a cast-iron storefront typical of these structures. Glue these parts together, as fig. 11-5 shows, but don't glue them to the rest of the structure.

You can now paint the two main subassemblies. I used an airbrush to paint the structure with Polly Scale Boxcar Red, but a brush or spray can would also do a good job. See the sidebar on page 78 for some tips on painting.

For the entryway subassembly I used Polly Scale Railroad Tie Brown. I wanted the doors to be a contrasting color, so I first masked them (fig. 11-6) before painting the rest of the piece brown.

You can also paint the roof now. I used a wide brush to paint it Polly Scale Grimy Black. I also painted the window frames white. Even though the windows were already molded in white, painting them will kill the plastic shine and improve their appearance.

Fig. 11-3. Use thick liquid plastic cement to join the corners of the structure.

Fig. 11-4. Adding a reinforcing strip of square styrene will stabilize corners.

Fig. 11-5. Glue all subassemblies (such as this lower storefront) together before painting.

Fig. 11-6. It's easy to make the doors a contrasting color by masking the doors before painting the rest of the subassembly.

Once the paint dries, you can glue the front in place on the structure. See fig. 11-7. Scrape any paint off the mating surfaces, and remember to use the glue sparingly—a little goes a long way.

Glue the window frames in place, as fig. 11-8 shows. I like to set the frames in place from behind, then touch the joints with liquid plastic cement.

Next add the window glazing. Many kits such as this one include glazing in the form of injection-molded clear styrene. Others include thin sheets of clear acetate or styrene. I used the supplied clear styrene for the storefront windows, as fig. 11-9 shows. The other pieces were warped, however, so I substituted .015″-thick clear styrene from Evergreen.

Don't use plastic cement for these parts—if any accidentally oozes out of the joint, it will be quite noticeable. Instead, use clear parts glue such as Model Master no. 8876. Use small drops, and keep the glue away from the opening if possible. If a bit of the glue oozes out, it will dry clear and glossy, so won't be very noticeable.

Window treatments come next. Figure 11-10 shows a quick, inexpensive way to dress up windows. You can simulate shades by gluing pieces of paper, thin cardstock, or construction paper behind the glazing. Cut the paper at different heights to represent shades that are fully drawn or partially open.

Glue them in place with clear parts glue, once again keeping the glue points well away from the visible areas of the windows.

You can now glue the roof in place. You'll still have access from the bottom of the building if you decide to dress up the

Fig. 11-7. Glue the subassemblies together. Make sure there's no paint on mating surfaces.

Fig. 11-8. Touching a brush of liquid cement to the window joint from behind lets capillary action pull the glue into the joint.

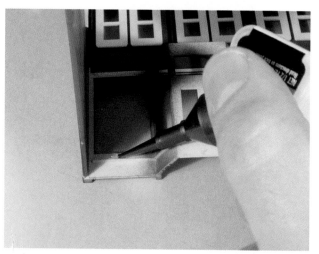

Fig. 11-9. Place clear parts glue sparingly on the inner wall around the windows, then add the clear plastic window glazing.

display windows in front. The design of some kits allows roofs to be removable—a handy feature if you add interior details. See fig. 11-11.

One problem with structures that don't have interior details or separate floors is that it's too easy for viewers to see through the building. Being able to look in through windows on one floor and see out the windows on another floor isn't very realistic.

Adding a viewblock solves this problem, as fig. 11-12 shows. Simply cut a piece of black construction paper as tall as the interior and slightly longer than the diagonal span of the building. This keeps viewers from seeing through, and the dull black paper soaks up light, making it difficult to see that the building doesn't have an interior.

Finish the structure with any necessary additional painting (fig. 11-13). This can include window frames and trim, chimneys, cornices, wall caps, vents, doorknobs, and other items. Figure 11-14 shows the finished building.

Wood kits

In the past most wood structures fell into the category of craftsman kits, and most parts required a great deal of cutting and fitting. Although many still fit this category, there are now many excellent wood kits on the market that are almost as easy to assemble as their plastic counterparts. These kits, from American Model Builders and others, have precut (often laser-cut) parts and tab-and-slot construction.

Figure 11-15 shows an AMB kit for a depot. Construction follows much the same order as a plastic kit. White glue works well for securing pieces, although medium-viscosity cyanoacrylate can also be used.

Wood pieces—especially large flat ones—are much more delicate than their plastic counterparts. If you break a piece, don't despair: Put a thin coat of white glue along the break and press the pieces next to each other on a piece of waxed paper. Weigh down the pieces if necessary to keep them flat while the glue dries.

Wood structures must be braced adequately to prevent warping when they're painted. Some kits provide this bracing; otherwise, strips of ⅛″- to ¼″-square stripwood glued behind walls is usually sufficient.

Signs and details

Structures are the easiest models to personalize. Doing this is fun and makes your building different from the thousands of otherwise identical kits out there.

Fig. 11-10. Create the appearance of window shades by gluing pieces of card or construction paper behind the windows.

Fig. 11-11. The roof on this Design Preservation Models depot is designed to be removable, a handy feature if you plan to add interior details.

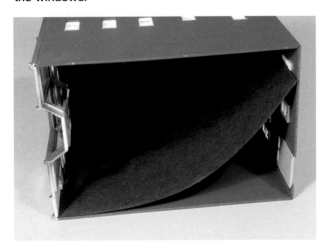

Fig. 11-12. A black construction-paper viewblock keeps viewers from seeing through the structure.

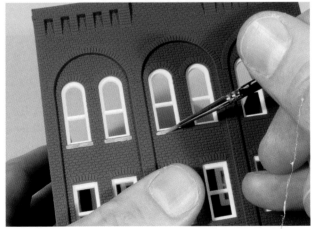

Fig. 11-13. Use a brush to paint any final details on the structure.

Fig. 11-14. The model is finished, awaiting signs and details.

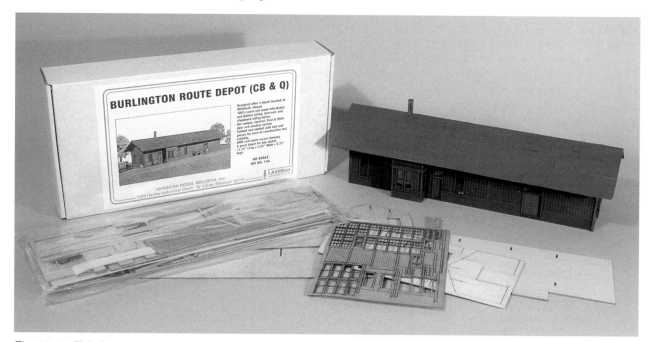

Fig. 11-15. This laser-cut wood kit features precut parts and tab-and-slot construction. Wood kits require painting.

Painting with brushes and spray cans

Although you'll hear from many experienced modelers that an airbrush is the only way to give a model a smooth paint finish, you can get very good results with a brush.

Stick with water-based paints, such as Polly Scale and Badger Modelflex. These cover and adhere well, they come in hundreds of colors, including many that are railroad-specific, and they don't have the health and cleanup problems of lacquer-based paints.

Choose as large a brush as practical for the job at hand. For structure walls this often means a ¼" or ½" flat brush. For details and smaller areas, a no. 0 or no. 1 will work well. Thoroughly wet the brush, then dry it with a cloth prior to painting. This will help keep paint from drying and sticking to the bristles, making cleanup much easier.

Dip just the tips of the bristles into the paint. Stroke the paint on the surface, following the direction of prominent surface features, such as horizontal brick lines or clapboard siding. When reloading the brush, apply paint in a new area, then brush it back into the still-wet area. This will minimize brushstrokes. Use as few strokes as possible—use only as many as it takes to apply the paint evenly.

Be sure the paint is completely dry before adding a second coat (a hair dryer on low works well for speeding the drying time of acrylics).

Camel-hair brushes are fine for most general paint work, including textured surfaces. When working on smooth surfaces, use a softer sable or synthetic brush. Remember that in general, the softer the brush, the fewer the brushstrokes and the smoother the finish will be.

Clean brushes in warm running water with a bit of liquid dish detergent, then rinse them thoroughly. Reshape the bristles while they're still wet, and store them with the bristles up. With proper care a good brush will last through years of modeling.

Spray cans

If you don't have access to an airbrush, a spray can will provide a smooth finish. Safety is very important when using spray paints: Only use them in well-ventilated areas, meaning either in a vented spray booth or outdoors. Spray paints contain solvents that can do serious damage to your lungs and central nervous system, so take all label warnings seriously.

Floquil and Scalecoat make spray paints specifically for model railroading, with colors to match real railroad colors. Other model spray paints are also available, including Testor's, Model Master, and Pactra. General-purpose spray paints, such as Krylon and others, can also work, but often the paint pigment isn't ground as finely as in model paints and so can result in a thicker paint coat. Just be sure to test new paints before trying them on a model.

Shake the can thoroughly for two minutes prior to use, and make sure the can is warm. If the can has been stored in a cool area (below 70 degrees), set it in a pan of warm (not hot) water for several minutes before using.

Test the spray on a piece of cardboard or other scrap before using it on your model. Begin spraying to the side of the model, then move it quickly across the surface. Don't release the nozzle until the spray pattern has cleared the side of the model.

Don't try to completely cover a model in one coat. Two or three light coats will yield a much better finish than a single heavy coat. Vary the spraying angle slightly with each coat to make sure that all details and raised areas have been thoroughly covered.

After each use tip the can upside down and spray until no paint comes out. This will clear the nozzle and keep it from clogging.

Allow spray-painted models to sit for at least 24 hours in a dust-free place before working with them. This allows the paint to cure.

Figure 11-16 shows how I decorated one storefront structure. Note that not much actual interior detail is necessary—in this case a small display shelf made from scrap styrene and a few fruit crate details from Preiser. Figure 11-17 shows an interior view of how this was done.

Signs add a great deal of life and realism to structures. The signs in fig. 11-16 came from a variety of sources. Figure 11-18 shows just a few of the hundreds of commercially available sign sets, made by companies like Bar Mills, Blair Line, JL Innovative Design, Microscale, and others.

Besides these commercial sources, keep your eyes open for old magazine advertisements, matchbook covers, catalogs, stationery, and packaging, all of which can be valuable sources for good signs.

If you have a computer with internet access, you can often find photos of old signs that can be downloaded and printed out. Also remember that if you can take a photo of a real sign, you can turn it into a sign for your layout either by taking the photo at the proper size, or by scanning it, resizing or otherwise altering it, and printing it out.

You can also add more elaborate interior detail to a structure, as shown with the Design Preservation Models café in fig. 11-19. The floor, walls, and counters are made from plain styrene that's been painted. The figures and tables (including plates and bottles) are from Preiser, and the signs are from a variety of sources.

Fig. 11-16. At first glance it looks highly detailed, but this Design Preservation Models building just has signs and a few simple details in its windows.

Fig. 11-17. Small styrene window shelves hold Preiser vegetable crates, creating the illusion of more extensive interior detail.

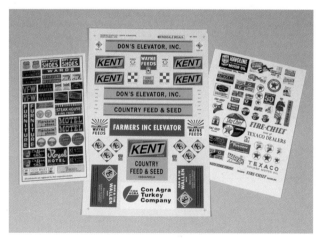

Fig. 11-18. Examples of the many signs available include these Blair Line signs, Microscale Decal signs, and JL Innovative Designs signs.

Fig. 11-19. Interior details in this Design Preservation Models building include Preiser tables and figures and signs from many manufacturers.

chapter twelve

Basic Scenery

Nothing makes a model railroad come alive—or turns a train set into a
real model railroad—like scenery. Unfortunately, scenery probably scares
more beginning modelers than any other facet of the hobby. This needn't
be the case. Basic scenery is easy to create—and re-create if need be.

I encourage you to jump in and try some. Start with a small area, and soon you'll have the confidence to tackle your whole layout. If some scenery doesn't turn out quite the way you wanted, just scrape it away and try again.

We'll take a look at some basic scenery techniques, using the water-soluble methods made popular by Dave Frary in his book *How to Build Realistic Model Railroad Scenery* (Kalmbach Publishng Co.). The basic idea is to apply various scenic materials in layers, using all water-based adhesives and paints to bond the materials. This ensures compatibility, and water-based products are safe to use.

The first step is to determine where you want structures, roads, bridges, and other scenic elements. These can always be added after scenery is in place, but it's easier if you can do it now. Figure 12-1 shows a simple scene on a tabletop.

Structures need some type of foundation or pad to give them a solid base and blend them into the scenery. Figure 12-2 shows how to make a simple base with cork roadbed. You can also use plywood, foam core, or extruded styrofoam cut to shape, depending upon the size and height you're looking for.

Scenic contours

To blend the structure bases into the scenery and to add some variation in elevation, you can add some material to the otherwise flat tabletop. Plaster has long been a favorite among modelers, but I prefer a material called Sculptamold. This powder product made by Amaco resembles plaster, but it is more fibrous and has more texture than plaster.

Sculptamold's biggest advantage is that it's less messy than plaster, which is prone to dripping. Sculptamold is also easier to shape into contours and is lighter than plaster.

To use Sculptamold, put a cup or two into a plastic mixing container, as fig. 12-3 shows. Gradually add water and stir it in until the mixture reaches a thick consistency, as in fig. 12-4. You don't want it to get soupy or watery, or it will be difficult to shape and take a long time to dry.

Spread it on the layout with a putty knife, your bare hands, or a kitchen spoon, as fig. 12-5 shows. I prefer a spoon because the back side of it works well for shaping and contouring. If the Sculptamold sticks to the spoon, wet the back of the spoon with water. Dampened fingers work well for getting a smooth texture.

Fig. 12-1. Before starting scenery, test various arrangements of structures, roads, and other details. The structures are from various manufacturers; the street sections are from Walthers.

Fig. 12-2. This building (a plaster kit from C.C. Crow) required a base to elevate it to track level. Strips of cork glued in place work well for this.

Fig. 12-3. Dry Sculptamold resembles plaster, but with more fiber content.

Fig. 12-4. Add water gradually and mix thoroughly until the Sculptamold reaches a fairly thick consistency like this. It shouldn't be runny.

Although the photos show Sculptamold on a flat surface, it also works well on hills and other contours. The sidebar below shows a couple of methods for making hills.

If you use plaster, the methods remain much the same. Mix plaster to a soupy consistency. Keep coats of plaster and Sculptamold fairly thin—no thicker than $1/4$″ or so. Thick coats can take significantly longer to dry, and—especially plaster—can crack when drying.

If you need to apply an additional coat, use a spray bottle to wet the Sculptamold or plaster that's already in place before adding the second coat. This will help the two layers bond to each other and will help keep the dry material from sucking all the moisture from the second coat.

Color and texture

If you haven't already covered the track with tape, do so now. Once you have the scenic contour where you want it, paint the surface with earth-colored flat latex paint (fig. 12-6). You don't need great paint for this—buy the least expensive brand you can find.

Fig. 12-5. Spread the Sculptamold on the layout with an old spoon or putty knife.

Hills and valleys

Hills are fairly easy to make, although they're a bit more advanced than basic scenery. These drawings show the basics. Step one is forming the hill itself. One popular method uses crumpled newspaper covered with either a web of masking tape or a web of cardboard strips hot-glued or stapled together. Wood blocks of various sizes support the strips.

Over this form goes a plaster shell that you can make in one of two ways. The traditional method is to use strips of paper towels dipped in plaster and placed on the contour. A modern method is to use plaster-impregnated gauze wrap (from Woodland Scenics and others). Although it's more expensive, the gauze is easy to use and less messy than plaster-soaked paper towels. Cut the wrap into strips, dip them in water, then lay them in place.

Once the shell hardens, you can add a thin coat of Sculptamold or plaster to provide an even surface. From there you can add your preferred ground cover as described in this chapter.

Another popular method is the use of extruded polystyrene insulation (pink or blue). As the drawing below shows, layers of this foam board can be stacked, then carved to shape using hot-wire tools, knives, saws, or other means. Scenery can be applied directly to the foam, or a layer of plaster or Sculptamold can be used for final contouring before applying scenery materials.

2. Weave in horizontal strips and staple (or hot glue) where strips cross. (Stapling is much faster and easier, but requires a pliers-type stapler.)

3. Lay on surface of hand-sized paper towel strips dipped in soupy plaster (messy method), or plaster cloth strips (neat method). Plaster cloth is sold in hobby shops.

4. Apply finish surface with putty knife, using plaster (messy), or Sculptamold (very neat). Sculptamold is sold in hobby and craft shops.

1. Hot glue vertical 1″-wide corrugated cardboard strips in place.

Fig. 1 MODELING SCENIC FORMS
A. Cardboard strip method

Increase flexibility by bending while pulling across a handy surface.

Cut strips across the corrugations.

Advantages	Disadvantages
1. Inexpensive (particularly with messy methods).	1. Need carefully applied finish layer to hide outline of strips.
2. Fast (particularly on broad expanses).	2. May need modifications to obtain final shape.
3. Easily modified.	3. Messy (unless plaster cloth and Sculptamold are used).
4. Lightweight (particularly if Sculptamold is used).	

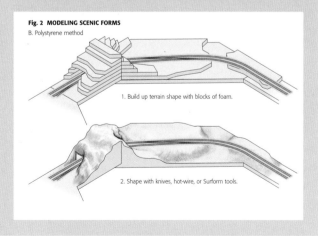

Fig. 2 MODELING SCENIC FORMS
B. Polystyrene method

1. Build up terrain shape with blocks of foam.

2. Shape with knives, hot-wire, or Surform tools.

Medium tan is a good choice to start with, but the color depends upon the area you're trying to model. Darker browns or soil (grimy black) colors can also work well.

Start with a fairly small area—a couple square feet at most. The key is to add the scenic texture materials while the paint is still wet, so the paint helps serve as a bonding agent.

Ground foam is the most commonly used material for creating grass and brush. There's a tremendous variety of textures and colors on the market from makers like Woodland Scenics, AMSI, Busch, Life-Like, Sunlit Vistas, and others.

Foam textures generally include fine, medium, and coarse, in colors from dark to light green as well as blends, soil and earth, and burnt and yellow grass. This variety allows you to use colors appropriate to the area you're modeling.

Ground cover generally comes packaged in bags or in plastic shaker-dispensers. See fig. 12-7. Old parmesan cheese containers are also very handy for sprinkling material. Be sure to label con-tainers so you know what's in them. If you buy the commercial shakers, you only need to buy one for each color once—then use the bagged material to refill them.

Sprinkle ground foam in place. See fig. 12-8. Start with fine textures and work up to coarse until you get the desired effect.

The wet paint will hold some of the initial material in place, but you'll need to bond the upper layers as well. An excellent way of doing this is with diluted white glue—about one part glue to three parts water. I like to mix the glue and water in an old mayonnaise jar, as fig. 12-9 shows. You'll need quite a bit of glue for even a small layout, so buying a gallon jug of glue is far more economical than buying smaller dispensers.

Once the glue is mixed, you'll need an applicator to dribble it in place. I tried using an eyedropper, but it's quite tedious to keep refilling and using the dropper. In my search for an alternative, I've found that old saline-solution bottles (for contact lenses) work beautifully. See fig. 12-9. If you don't have access to them, ask a

Fig. 12-6. Paint the layout surface with a fairly heavy coat of earth-colored flat latex paint.

Fig. 12-7. Ground cover is available in shaker bottles and bags from Woodland Scenics, Sunlit Vistas, Scenic Express, and others.

Fig. 12-8. Old parmesan cheese containers work well for sprinkling ground foam onto the wet paint.

Fig. 12-9. Mix white glue and water in a large con-tainer, such as an old mayonnaise jar. Old contact lens solution bottles work very well for dispensing the mix. Woodland Scenics Scenic Glue dries flat, so it is a good choice when you need full-strength glue for glu-ing foliage in place.

friend who wears contacts—you'll soon have a ready supply.

Applying this mix directly to the scenery won't work—it won't soak in. You need to soak the scenery to allow the glue mixture to penetrate.

I prefer using rubbing alcohol, although the old standby of water with a few drops of liquid dish detergent also will work. A small spray bottle, like the old hair spray bottle in fig. 12-10, works for applying it. When choosing a spray bottle, find one that sprays with an extremely fine mist. Small pump-type bottles like this hair-spray bottle fit the bill better than trigger-type bottles, which tend to spray larger drops that disturb the scenery materials.

I prefer alcohol over the water/detergent mix for several reasons: The alcohol soaks in more readily, helping the glue mix penetrate better. The alcohol spray won't disturb the ground foam as much as water. Alcohol also evaporates faster than water—your scenery will dry more quickly.

Spray the ground cover with rubbing alcohol, as in fig. 12-10. Make sure the scenery is wet, but without puddles.

Next, use the applicator to drip the white glue/water mix over the scenery. See fig. 12-11. If the glue starts to bead up or doesn't soak in readily, spray some more alcohol on the area. Be sure to saturate the area completely with the glue mix.

When the glue is applied, the scenery will look milky and mottled—it won't much resemble what it looked like when you applied it. This is normal, so don't worry—as the glue dries, the white will fade away and the scenery will regain its appearance.

Other texture options

There are other options besides ground foam. If you're aiming for the look of individual blades of grass, such as in a well-kept lawn or park, take a look at electrostatic grass.

Figure 12-12 shows how to apply static grass (I used Noch; other brands are also available). You can start by painting the ground area and adding the grass directly to it, but I prefer to start with a layer of fine ground foam, gluing it in place with diluted glue as described earlier.

Apply the static grass while the glue on the ground foam is still wet. This is done by "poofing" the applicator bottle while holding

Fig. 12-10. Spray the ground cover with rubbing alcohol. Small pump-type bottles work well because they spray in a very fine mist.

Fig. 12-11. Use the lens solution bottle or other applicator to soak the ground cover thoroughly with the diluted glue mix.

Fig. 12-12. Apply static grass by squeezing the applicator bottle directly above the glue-soaked ground. Static electricity will pull the grass fibers upright.

Fig. 12-13. The finished static grass has the look of a nicely maintained lawn.

it above the scenery, as fig. 12-12 shows. The plastic bottle gives the grass a static charge, causing the grass fibers to stand up. Figure 12-13 shows the results.

Real dirt, gravel, and rocks are also very effective to use, because they can capture colors and textures sometimes not possible with artificial materials.

Old coffee cans or ice cream containers are handy for filling with these materials. I collect black dirt for fields, gravel of various colors for roads, parking lots, and highway shoulders, and small twigs for simulating trees and logs.

Quite often real dirt and gravel aren't fine enough to use on a layout. To make them more usable, sift them through a piece of old aluminum window screen, as fig. 12-14 shows. You can repeat the process with finer screen to get various grades of material.

I used some dirt (taken from my garden) to make a plowed field along the front of the scene. To do this, start by painting the surface, as you did with other scenery. In this case, however, I used flat black paint to go with the dark dirt. Sprinkle ground foam to fill in the area between the tracks and the edge of the field.

While the paint is still wet, use a cup to sprinkle dirt in the area of the field, as fig. 12-15 shows. Pat it down with your fingers to ensure that it bonds well to the paint, then leave it alone until the paint dries.

Make a tool for shaping the furrows using an old comb. Use a hobby knife to remove every other tooth on the coarse side of the comb. The resulting tooth spacing is about right for HO scale furrows.

Drag the comb slowly along the dirt, as in fig. 12-16. It will probably take several passes to create the impression of furrows. Once the field looks the way you want, spray it with alcohol and bond it like ground foam.

Ballasting track

Main lines generally have well-maintained crushed rock ballast of various shades of gray, white, salt-and-pepper, or reddish stones. Branch lines and industrial spurs often have cinders for ballast, with roadbed contour that's often not as apparent. Grass and weeds often intrude into the ballast itself. This visual contrast

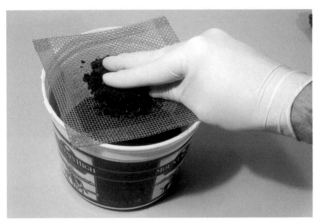

Fig. 12-14. Sift dirt and other natural materials through aluminum window screen. Rubber gloves will keep your hands clean.

Fig. 12-15. Sprinkle the sifted dirt onto the wet black paint, then press it in place.

Fig. 12-16. Create furrows by dragging an old comb (with alternate teeth removed) across the dirt.

is very realistic when you capture it on your model railroad.

I like to add ballast to track after the surrounding ground textures are all in place. This decreases the chance of getting ground foam and other materials on the track and ballast.

Ballast is available in many textures and colors from Woodland Scenics, Arizona Rock & Mineral, and others. Medium texture works well for HO, although fine is also appropriate.

Figure 12-17 shows how to spread ballast on the track. Use a small cup to spread ballast first between the rails. Use a $\frac{1}{2}$″ or $\frac{3}{4}$″ flat brush to distribute the ballast evenly between the ties. See fig. 12-18.

Spread ballast on the sides next, starting with the ends of the ties and moving to the slope. See fig. 12-19. Use a smaller brush to do any final adjusting of the ballast, getting stray rocks off ties where you don't want them.

Take care around turnouts to make sure ballast (and later glue) doesn't interfere with moving parts. Spread ballast carefully around the turnout, as fig. 12-20 shows, making sure the ballast in the point area is below rail level. Check by moving the points back and forth. Make sure there's no ballast in the guard rails or flangeways through the frog.

If you use above-ground switch machines, mask them before bonding your ballast. Don't install below-table machines until after the ballast has been bonded (or remove them during the

Fig. 12-17. Use a small cup to sprinkle ballast between the rails.

Fig. 12-18. Use a soft, flat brush to distribute the ballast evenly between the ties.

Fig. 12-19. Add ballast on the sides, using just enough to cover the cork roadbed.

Fig. 12-20. Make sure that ballast in and around turnouts doesn't interfere with the points, flangeways, or throw bar.

process), or glue can easily seep through and damage the machine.

Spray the ballast with rubbing alcohol, starting with a fine, light mist to hold the material in place, followed by a heavy coat. It's important that the ballast be saturated completely, or the glue won't penetrate. The result will be a thin shell of bonded ballast, which will eventually crack.

Follow this with a thorough application of diluted white glue, as fig. 12-21 shows. Once the glue has been added, use a damp cotton swab to remove as much of it as possible from the ties under the turnout point rails. See fig. 12-22. As the glue dries, periodically move the points of turnouts back and forth to make sure they don't become stuck.

To add ballast on the seldom-used spur track, I mixed some Woodland Scenics fine cinder ballast with some fine dark green ground foam. Spread this mix on the track, as fig. 12-23 shows. Don't be particular about the contour—note how some of the ties are completely covered, while others are in plain view.

Completing the scene

The basic scene is now complete. The street is made from Walthers Cornerstone street sections, glued to the plywood with cyanoacrylate. To hide any gaps between the street and scenery, and to help structures blend with the scenery, run a bead of glue along their edges and add ground foam, as fig. 12-24 shows. You

Fig. 12-21. After soaking the ballast with rubbing alcohol, apply a heavy coat of diluted white glue.

Fig. 12-22. Use a damp cotton swab to soak up glue from the ties under the turnout points.

Fig. 12-23. Ground foam can be mixed with ballast to model spurs and other seldom-used tracks.

can use white glue for this, but I prefer Woodland Scenics Scenic Glue because it dries flat, making it nearly invisible once it dries.

Figure 12-25 shows the scene after the basic scenery is complete.

Now comes the fun part—adding the finishing touches that make a layout come alive. The photos on pages 5 and 80 show the scene after adding additional details, which included telegraph poles from Rix with lines made from Berkshire Junction's E-Z Line; figures from Preiser; signs from Blair Line; vehicles from Mini-Metals and Walthers; streetlights from Woodland Scenics; and trees from Life-Like, Woodland Scenics, and Sunlit Vistas. The fence along the field is made from square toothpicks cut to length, painted various colors, and planted in holes drilled in the layout.

Use your imagination when detailing a scene, as there are thousands of parts and accessories available, depending upon the region, era, and railroad you model. You can also make alterations—note that I decided to add a parking lot at the end of the Gamble Robinson building because the area looked too plain. Some gravel and glue, and the scene was ready.

Making basic scenery and adding details is relatively easy, fun to do, and goes a long way toward making your layout look real.

I've taken you as far as possible in a single book. I encourage

Fig. 12-24. Hide gaps by running a bead of Scenic Glue along the gap, then pressing ground foam in place.

you to read and study other books on scenery, structures, operation, wiring, and other areas of the hobby. More important, though, is your willingness to experiment with various techniques. Don't be afraid if something doesn't turn out as planned. Keep trying, and above all, keep having fun!

Fig. 12-25. The basic scene is now finished—all that's left are the details.

Trackside Photos

A Burlington Northern Santa Fe manifest freight led by a former Santa Fe GP60 rolls through town on Pelle Søeborg's 2 x 9-foot HO scale diorama. Many of the techniques Pelle used can be easily adapted to building a small model railroad. Pelle Søeborg

In the remaining pages you'll tour a gallery of model railroad photos.

Model railroading is such a rich hobby that we can only hint at its variety.

Old time steam, powerful new diesels, rugged mountains, colorful

deserts—any railroad possibility you can think of is the special interest of

some modeler, somewhere.

(Above) Dave Rickaby's HO scale Wisconsin & Michigan Western Division features railroading with a purpose. Here, westbound manifest train 23 crosses the bridge over Giggling Squaw Creek and arrives at Mole Lake Yard just as an empty hopper train departs. Dave Rickaby

(Right) Ten-Wheeler no. 2605 backs up to a spur to switch the feed mill in the small farming community of Stockton. All this takes place on the late John Proebsting's HO scale Soo Line. John Proebsting

(Left) A Barre & Chelsea GE 70-tonner no. 14 switches granite loads at Barrett, N. H., on Paul Dolkos' HO scale layout.
Paul Dolkos

(Below) Bob Smaus uses a little ingenuity to disguise trains passing through holes in the backdrop of his HO scale Southern Pacific set in Los Angeles. Bob Smaus

gallery

(Right) Missouri Pacific 2-10-2 no. 1517 has just left Bluff City Yard, as it rumbles across the Mississippi River bridge into Arkansas on its southbound trip to Forrest City on Allen Keller's HO scale Bluff City Southern. Lou Sassi

(Below) The essence of pool power is displayed as a B&M GP38, an NER GP40, and a Guilford/Maine Central GP38 drag this heavy grain train through State Line Tunnel at Berkshire Junction. This contemporary scenario takes place on the Nashua Valley Railroad Association's HO scale New England Rail System layout. Lou Sassi

(Above) Ron Furto took his 2 x 4-foot diorama outdoors for this shoot of two Rock Island Alco Century 415 center-cab units heading up a transfer run on an elevated line. Ron Furto

(Left) With the help of several friends, Mike Shanahan was able to recreate the exciting operations of the Pennsylvania RR in the 1950s on his HO scale Brunswick & Tuscan RR. Here, Pennsy K4s no. 8219 speeds an eastbound passenger train past the Easy Washer Co.
Mike Shanahan

(Right) As the CSX GE Dash 8-44CW pulls its train of covered hoppers over a double-track crossing, it slips past a color position light signal, a reminder of the railroad's history. HO scale modeling by Gary Hoover. Gary Hoover

(Above left) A few inches of snow isn't enough to slow this Denver & Rio Grande Western piggyback train gliding through Winter Park, Colo., and up the west flank of the Rocky Mountains to Moffat Tunnel. The Southern Pacific units trailing lead GP40-2 3123 reflect the recently completed merger of the D&RGW and SP. HO scale modeling by Doug Tagsold. Doug Tagsold

(Left) Time is precious for this Boston & Maine E7 as it heads west across State Route 20 out of Adams, Mass., with the daily milk train. Lou Sassi, author of *Basic Scenery for Model Railroaders* (Kalmbach) did the modeling and took the photo. Don Janes detailed and painted the HO scale locomotive. Lou Sassi

Suppliers and manufacturers

Accurail
P. O. Box 278, Elburn, IL 60119
www.accurail.com

A-Line/Proto Power West
P. O. Box 2701, Carlsbad, CA 92018
www.ppw-aline.com

American Model Builders
1420 Hanley Industrial Ct., St. Louis, MO 63144
www.laserkit.com

Arizona Rock & Mineral
P. O. Box 567, Paulden, AZ 86334
www.rrscenery.com

Athearn Inc.
19010 Laurel Park Rd., Compton, CA 90220
www.athearn.com

Atlas Model Railroad Co.
378 Florence Ave., Hillside, NJ 07205
www.atlasrr.com

Aztec Manufacturing Co.
2701 Conestoga Dr., No. 113, Carson City, NV 89706
www.aztectrains.com

Bachmann Trains
1400 E. Erie Ave., Philadelphia, PA 19124
www.bachmanntrains.com

Bar Mills Scale Model Works
P. O. Box 609, Bar Mills, ME 04004
www.barmillsmodels.com

Blair Line
P. O. Box 1136, Carthage, MO 64836
www.blairline.com

Bowser Manufacturing
P. O. Box 322, Montoursville, PA 17754

Branchline Trains
333 Park Ave., E. Hartford, CT 06108
www.brainchline-trains.com

Broadway Limited Imports
P.O. Box 376, Ivy, VA 22945
www.broadway-limited.com

Centerline Products Inc.
18409 Harmony Rd., Marengo, IL 60152
www.centerline-products.com

Chooch Enterprises
P. O. Box 217, Redmond, WA 98052
www.choochenterprises.com

Circuitron (Tortoise)
211 RocBaar Dr., Romeoville, IL 60446
www.circuitron.com

C.C. Crow
10413 Marine View Dr., Mukiltoe, WA 98275
www.cccrow.com

CVP Products
P. O. Box 835772, Richardson, TX 75083
www.cvpusa.com

Digitrax Inc.
450 Cemetary St., No. 206, Norcross, GA 30071
www.digitrax.com

Eurorails Model Importer Ltd.
1000 S. Main St., Newark, NY 14513
www.ermodels.com

IBL Products
5452 Cascade Dr., West Bend, WI 53095
www.IBLProducts.com

InterMountain Railway
P. O. Box 839, Longmont, CO 80501
www.intermountain-railway.com

International Hobby Corp.
413 E. Allegheny Ave., Philadelphia, PA 19134
www.IHC-Hobby.com

JL Innovative Design Scale Models
P. O. Box 322, Sauk Rapids, MN 56379
www.jlinnovative.com

Kadee Quality Products
673 Avenue C, White City, OR 97503
www.kadee.com

Kato U.S.A.
100 Remington Rd., Schaumburg, IL 60173
www.katousa.com

LaBelle Industries
8101 E. Research Ct., Tucson, AZ 85710
www.all-railroads.com

Lenz Agency of North America
P. O. Box 143, Chelmsford, MA 01824
www.lenz.com

Life-Like Products LLC
1600 Union Ave., Baltimore, MD 21211
www.lifelikeproducts.com

Micro-Mark Precision Tools
340 Snyder Ave., Berkeley Heights, NJ 07922
www.micromark.com

Microscale Industries
18435 Bandilier Circle, Fountain Valley, CA 92708
www.microscale.com

Midwest Products Co. Inc.
P. O. Box 564, Hobart, IN 46342
www.midwestproducts.com

Model Die Casting
5070 Sigstrom Dr., Carson City, NV 89706
www.mdcroundhouse.com

Model Power
180 Smith St., Farmingdale, NY 11735
www.modelpower.com

Model Rectifier Corp.
P. O. Box 6312, Edison, NJ 08818
www.modelrectifier.com

Noch (imported by Wm. K. Walthers)

NorthWest Short Line
P. O. Box 423, Seattle, WA 98111
www.nwsl.com

Overland Models
3808 W. Kilgore Ave., Muncie, IN 47304
www.overlandmodels.com

Peco (imported by Wm. K. Walthers)

REBOXX
7 Kane Industrial Dr., Hudson, MA 01749
www.reboxx.com

Red Caboose
P. O. Box 250, Mead, CO 80524
www.red-caboose.com

Rivarossi (imported by Wm. K. Walthers)

Roco (imported by Wm. K. Walthers)

Roundhouse (see Model Die Casting)

Stewart Hobbies
140 New Britain Blvd., Chalfont, PA 18914
www.stewarthobbies.com

Switchmaster/Builders In Scale (see C.C. Crow)

Testor Corp. (Floquil, Polly S, Model Master)
440 Blackhawk Park Ave., Rockford, IL 61104
www.testors.com

Tichy Train Group
P. O. Box 39, Plainview, NY 11803

Wm. K. Walthers
P. O. Box 3039, Milwaukee, WI 53201
www.walthers.com

Woodland Scenics
P. O. Box 98, Linn Creek, MO 65052
www.woodlandscenics.com

X-Acto/Hunt Corp.
2005 Market St., Philadelphia, PA 19103

Xuron Corp.
62 Industrial Park Rd., Saco, ME 04072
www.xuron.com

Index

Adhesives, 15

Ballasting track, 86-87
Benchwork
    Cookie-cutter top, 41, 43
    Shelf-style, 43
    Tables, 42, 43

Couplers
    Coupler gauge, 20
    Delayed action, 19
    Fine tuning, 20-21, 22
    Horn-hook, 18
    Installation, 21-22
    Knuckle, 18-19
    Locomotive mounting, 23
Cutting parts from sprues, 35

Digital Command Control (DCC), 62-64

Electrical basics, 60-61

Freight cars
    Adding loads to, 40
    Assembling kits, 34-38
    Quality of, 10
    Weighting, 38, 39

Glues, 15
Grades, 43

Hobby knives, 13

Locomotives
    Maintaining, 30-32
    Quality of, 9
    Steam locomotives, 31-32

Painting, 38, 74, 78

Pin vise, 14
Power packs, 60

Rail gaps, 52
Roadbed
    Cork, 44-46
    Under turnouts, 45-46

Scale and gauge, 8
Scale rules, 13
Scenery
    Ground cover, 83-85
    Hills and landforms, 82
    Sculptamold, applying, 81
Sprue cutters, 15
Structures
    Assembling kits, 73-76
    Detailing, 76, 79
    Painting, 74, 78
Switch machines, 56, 66

Tools
    Basic set, 12-13
    Safety, 16
Track
    All-in-one, 49
    Cleaning, 57
    Codes, 48
    Flextrack, 48, 53
    Laying, 50-53
    Painting, 54
    Prototype, 49
    Sectional, 48
    Turnouts, 55-56, 64, 66
Train sets
    Basics of, 8, 9
    Assembling your own, 11
Trucks
    Equalized, 27
    Fine tuning, 28
    Installing, 27
    Roller-bearing, 27
    Solid-bearing, 25

Uncoupling ramps, 19

Weathering with chalk, 39
Wheels and wheelsets
    Cleaning, 28, 32
    Fixing gauge, 26
    Sizes, 25
    Types, 26
Wire feeders, 52
Wiring
    Cab control, 60-61
    Control panels, 67
    Digital Command Control, 62-64
    Multimeters, 69
    Reverse loops, 64
    Soldering, 69-70
    Switch machines, 66-68
    Wire, 69

WITHDRAWN